THE HISTORY OF THE UNITED STATES FLAG

THE HISTORY

FROM THE REVOLUTION TO

ILLUSTRATED

Original drawings by Elmo Jones

HARPER & ROW, PUBLISHERS
NEW YORK, EVANSTON, AND LONDON

OF THE UNITED STATES FLAG

THE PRESENT, INCLUDING A GUIDE TO ITS USE AND DISPLAY

by Milo M. Quaife, Melvin J. Weig, and Roy E. Appleman

WITH CONTRIBUTIONS BY CHARLES E. SHEDD, JOHN A. HUSSEY, AND GEORGE C. MACKENZIE

FOREWORD BY ROGER BUTTERFIELD

PUBLISHED IN CO-OPERATION WITH THE
EASTERN NATIONAL PARK AND MONUMENT ASSOCIATION,
420 CHESTNUT STREET, PHILADELPHIA 6, PENNSYLVANIA

THE HISTORY OF THE UNITED STATES FLAG

Printed in the United States of America

Library of Congress catalog card number: 61-6428

For all Americans
who with pride, courage
and devotion have honored the
Stars and Stripes

CONTENTS

ILLUSTRATIONS

Plates

Black-and-White Drawings

FOREWORD

THIS BOOK PRESENTS, IN ATTRACTIVE PICTURES AND reliable text, the known facts about the origin and development of our national flag. It tells a remarkable and, in some respects, an almost incredible story. For those who prefer historical truth it will be a far more satisfying story than the fictions and wishful thinking that have given rise to so many "flag myths." It appears that the flag, like the nation itself, evolved slowly and painfully from small beginnings; that it was shaped by many hands and brains; and that only very recently has it been stabilized in an official design. Even now the flag is subject to change—the admission of two young States in the last few years has made it new again.

So much love, patriotism, and sacrifice are symbolized in the flag that it is hard for present-day Americans to realize that it did not have some dramatic moment of birth. Yet no one can say with certainty who first proposed the familiar design, or where and when the Stars and Stripes was first unfurled. What is definitely known is that General George Washington, on New Year's Day of 1776, displayed over his camp outside Boston an improvised "Grand Union Flag" which combined British and American features. The blue union in the upper corner bore the two familiar crosses—St. George for England and St. Andrew for Scotland—which had long been part of the British emblem, but the field had thirteen red and white stripes to represent the American colonies. Since the fighting colonists, including Washington, still claimed to be subjects of the British Crown, it was natural that their flag should carry token evidence of their loyalty.

The earliest historical mention of an independent flag is in a resolution of the Continental Congress dated June 14, 1777. This directs that "the flag of the United States be made of thirteen stripes, alternate red and white; the union be thirteen stars, white in a blue field, representing a new constellation." This was an obvious adaptation of Washington's "Grand Union Flag." Congress, however, laid down no specific rules about arrangement, size, or other details and it failed to supply Washington's army with official Stars and Stripes flags until 1783, when all the big battles were over. Meanwhile the American Army and Navy fought under a confused array of local, State and home-made flags adorned with pine and palmetto trees, rattlesnakes, eagles, red, blue and yellow stripes, blue and gold stars, and other variations.

In fact it was not until 1814, nearly forty years after the flag was authorized, that it began to be widely talked about and popular. The story of how a British Admiral, a poetic lawyer from Washington, and a singing actor on a Baltimore stage helped create "The Star-Spangled Banner" and make it our national anthem is told with some detail in this book. It marks the real beginning of national devotion to the flag. Four years after the song was written, in 1818, an obscure Tammany politician—whose name is here rescued from oblivion—forced his largely indifferent colleagues in Congress to pass a new bill which gave the flag a practical design. Until that time the flag makers had been adding a stripe as well as a star for every new State.

The authors of this book are to be congratulated for disentangling fact from fancy, for their careful analysis of the many false stories that have grown up around the flag, and for bringing to light much new and interesting history. From the day when John Paul Jones defiantly hoisted "the American stars" just off the coast of England to the moment when it was raised under fire by Marines on Iwo Jima, the flag has inspired countless deeds of glory. Its true life story, as set forth here, deserves to be well known.

ROGER BUTTERFIELD

PREFACE

THE IDEA FOR THIS BOOK ORIGINATED SEVERAL YEARS ago with the Eastern National Park and Monument Association, which considered it desirable to have available a compact but accurate publication on the American Flag. It was felt that such a work would appeal to visitors in the National Historical Parks and Monuments, where the Association co-operates with the National Park Service, United States Department of the Interior, in furthering improved interpretation of significant area features and values.

The Board of Directors of the Association accordingly referred this proposed project to the attention of its Publications Committee, then consisting of Mr. Roy E. Appleman (chairman), Historian, Branch of History, Washington Office of the National Park Service; Mr. Melvin J. Weig, Superintendent, Edison Laboratory National Monument, West Orange, New Jersey; and Mr. George F. Emery, Assistant Superintendent, Colonial National Historical Park, Yorktown, Virginia. Mr. Emery was subsequently succeeded by Mr. Charles E. Shedd, Jr., Historian, National Survey of Historic Sites and Buildings, assigned to the Region Five Office of the National Park Service in Philadelphia. This committee reviewed existing literature on the subject of the Stars and Stripes, but soon concluded that nothing available was either sufficiently comprehensive or up-to-date.

The committee then approached Dr. Milo M. Quaife, prominent historian and author of *The Flag of the United States* (New York: 1942), which although out of print appeared to be the most scholarly research production on the Stars and Stripes published up to that time. At their request, Dr. Quaife agreed to prepare a new study of the scope and type desired. In due course he submitted a manuscript, based largely on his previous work, for consideration by the Association.

Following preliminary review of this manuscript by its Publications Committee, the Association formally accepted Dr. Quaife's work. Mr. Weig then agreed to serve as general editor of the new book, and Mr. Appleman undertook to arrange for preparation of appropriate illustrations and related supplementary materials. As the work went forward, however, its overall extent was gradually enlarged, including major extensions of the text, reference notes, and pictorial features. The recent admission of Alaska and Hawaii to Statehood in the Federal Union also complicated the problem and made necessary still other additions and modifications. Shortly before the revised and expanded manuscript was ready for publication, Dr. Quaife was killed in an automobile accident in the autumn of 1959, and accordingly he was unable to review the final product before it went to press.

Part I of the book as here published was prepared mainly by Dr. Quaife, though his original manuscript has been much edited and enlarged, and some of his conclusions to a degree modified. Besides serving as general editor for the entire study, Mr. Weig also prepared Chapters 5 and 13 in Part I, based mainly on his own research, and with Dr. Quaife contributed the section on "The Code of Flag Display and Use" in Part V, besides adding much other material to the text and notes for Part I.

The task of arranging for the many illustrations was performed chiefly by Mr. Appleman, who selected Mr. Elmo Jones, an artist of Richmond, Virginia, to prepare the great majority of color plates and black-and-white drawings of various flags included in the book. Mr. Appleman likewise prepared the captions for these illustrations, which in numerous instances required considerable research. In addition, he undertook the necessary investigation and prepared Chapters 14 and 15 in Part II and all but one of the eight sections in Parts IV and V.

Mr. Shedd prepared Chapters 16 and 19 in Part III, assisted in obtaining certain illustrations, and as a member of the Publications Committee contributed unusually valuable editorial advice.

Other members of the National Park Service whose assistance is gratefully acknowledged are Mr. George C. Mackenzie, Historian, Fort McHenry National Monument and Historic Shrine, Baltimore, Maryland, who prepared that part of Chapter 7 in Part I which relates to the original Star-Spangled Banner; and Dr. John A. Hussey, Regional Historian, Region Four Office, San Francisco, California, who prepared Chapter 17 in Part III.

Except for the contributions of Dr. Quaife and Mr. Jones, whose original manuscript and drawings were purchased by the Eastern National Park and Monument Association, all editorial and other work in connection with preparation of this book has been entirely voluntary, without monetary compensation of any kind. The Association is especially indebted to Melvin J. Weig and Roy E. Appleman for their labors in bringing the project to completion.

HERBERT E. KAHLER, President
Eastern National Park and Monument Association

Washington, D. C.
February 22, 1961

Post Script

For the second edition of *The History of the United States Flag,* which incorporates the story and an illustration of the Hawaiian flag, the Eastern National Park and Monument Association is indebted to Frederick B. Wichman and A.E.P. Wall of Hilo, Hawaii; Hawaii Visitors Bureau, Bishop Museum and Bishop Museum Press of Honolulu; and Miss Agnes C. Conrad, State Archivist of Hawaii.

H.E.K.

Part I

THE ORIGIN AND HISTORIC DEVELOPMENT OF THE STARS AND STRIPES

Introduction

By the autumn of 1863 the American Civil War, then more than two years old, was approaching its climax. Every effort of the Union Government to conquer the Southern Confederacy had failed. Each report of fresh disaster added to the burdens of President Lincoln. As always at such times, doubt and despair overcame the faint-hearted, and the ranks of those for peace-at-any-price grew stronger daily. At this critical juncture, Edward Everett Hale wrote and published *The Man Without a Country,* to serve as a warning to the disloyal and an inspiration to all true-hearted Americans.

Hale's narrative was entirely fictional,[1]* but thousands of readers then and since have thrilled to the sad story of young Lieutenant Nolan, who in a moment of anger cursed his country and expressed the rash wish never to hear its name again. Taken at his word, as the account relates, he was committed to the custody of the United States Navy, and sentenced to have that wish fulfilled. More than half a century later, when Nolan was old, broken, and dying, and the ban was briefly lifted, his first eager inquiry was to know the identity of the seventeen stars which had been added to the American Flag in the interval of his terrible sentence.

For to Lieutenant Nolan, in the depth of his mind and soul, that flag was the outstanding symbol of his country. Though actually only a bit of silk or bunting in red, white, and blue colors, many thousands of Americans, both before and after his time, have given their lives in its defense. Strange as it seems, however, the true story of the Stars and Stripes is little known. Instead, there has developed about the flag a volume of myth and tradition which, by force of frequent repeti-

* Superior figures refer to a section of notes beginning on p. 179.

tion in numerous histories, popular addresses, movie films, and radio and television programs, has unfortunately been impressed upon the public mind as actual history.[2] This is a great pity, for the simple facts are more dignified and inspiring than any fanciful narrative could possibly be. To relate these, briefly and simply, is the purpose of the present volume.

PLATE I

1
English Cross of St. George

2
Scottish Cross of St. Andrew

3
British Union Flag as proclaimed by King James I in 1606, and used until 1801 except during Cromwell's time

4
British Union Jack, 1801

5
British Meteor Flag (Naval), 1705-1801

Plate II

6
Traditional Bunker Hill Flag,
Revolutionary War

7
Flag of the Hanover Association,
Revolutionary War

8
Flag of the Bedford Company,
Battle of Concord,
Revolutionary War

9
Flag of the First Troop, Philadelphia City Cavalry. This flag is yellow silk, with silver fringe. The canton in its corner carries 13 alternate blue and silver stripes. It is the first known instance of an American banner carrying 13 stripes. The flag is approximately 3 feet by 3½ feet in size. Captain Abraham Markoe in 1775 presented the original flag to the Philadelphia Troop of Light Horse, subsequently known as the First Troop, Philadelphia City Cavalry. The troop carried the flag at the battles of Trenton, Princeton, Brandywine, and Germantown. The First City Troop preserves the original in its Philadelphia armory.

CHAPTER 1 ★

Before the Stars and Stripes

A FLAG IS A SYMBOL OF PERSONS UNITED IN SOME common association. The highest form of such group unity is the sovereign state. Nearly every person belongs to some state, to which he owes allegiance, and the national flag serves as a ready means of identifying his connection. Particularly at sea, or in warfare on land or in the air, this becomes an urgent matter. Flags and uniforms have been developed to serve this purpose, and all countries recognize a code of rules governing their usage.

Although the national flag as we have it today is of comparatively recent development, symbols of some kind were employed in warfare from the dawn of recorded history. "Terrible as an army with banners" fell from the lips of Solomon three thousand years ago. For many centuries flags and their kindred devices served merely as symbols of authority of the king or other military leader who displayed them. Indeed, the royal standard is still the personal emblem of the monarch, being displayed, for example, over his palace when he actually occupies it. In like fashion the American President has his special flag, which is flown from his ship when he undertakes a voyage, and is even displayed on the launch which conveys him from dock to vessel. In the later Middle Ages, however, a group of independent city states grew up in Italy. Since these had no king or other personal ruler, they evolved the idea of a flag to symbolize the state itself.

One of such states was Genoa, which obtained a guarantee of separate communal rights in A.D. 958. St. George was adopted as the patron saint of the city at some later date, and about the year 1100 the flag of St. George, white with a broad red cross upon its field, came into use.

St. George was a Roman soldier of the third century A.D. about whom we know very little, except that he met death as a Christian martyr, and is the hero of the legendary feat of slaying the dragon. Perhaps for these reasons his memory remained green long afterward, and when the English Crusaders came to Italy his story captivated them. They carried it back to England, where gradually the red cross of St. George displaced earlier banners (Plate I-1). In 1386, for example, all the men whom King Richard II led against the Scots were commanded to wear the red cross upon their clothing, both in front and rear. In like fashion, their Scottish enemies displayed the white cross of St. Andrew "before and behind" (Pl. I-2).

On the death of Queen Elizabeth I in 1603, the royal line of Tudor rulers came to an end, and James VI of Scotland was invited to occupy the vacant English throne. Thus the two kingdoms, which for centuries had been bitter rivals, became united under his personal rule. But deep-seated jealousies persisted, and particularly at sea quarrels over issues like precedence and honors were constant.

To end such bickering, King James in 1606 created the Union Flag, which combined the crosses of St. George and St. Andrew, ordering both English and Scottish vessels, upon meeting, to display this emblem at their maintop (Pl. I-3). English ships would also fly the cross of St. George in their foretop, while Scottish vessels were to display "the white cross of St. Andrew only, as they were accustomed."[1]

There followed a century of dynastic upheaval, revolution, and warfare, with corresponding changes in the use of flags by the two kingdoms until they were permanently joined by the Act of Union in 1707. The Union Flag was retained, and, somewhat modified by addition of the Irish cross of St. Patrick in 1801, it still flies over British subjects around the world (Pl. I-4).

One further flag remains to be noted. Early in the seventeenth century it became customary for ships in the Royal Navy to fly a small banner on the bowsprit. This was called the Jack, and in the beginning it was a small edition of the earlier Union Flag.[2] As time passed, however, it evolved into a red flag with the union in its first canton, that is, in the upper left-hand quarter of the field, the position occupied in the American Flag by the stars (Pl. I-5). From 1707 on, both this new "Meteor" Flag and the Union Flag remained in common use. Both were developed, as we have seen, for use at sea.

The United States is the offspring of Great Britain, and the story of its flag is closely interwoven with that of the mother country. For a century and a half, the American colonies shared Britain's flags, the Union and the red Meteor banners being familiar sights in all their coastal harbors.

The close of the Seven Years' War (1756-63) left France prostrate and England triumphant on land and sea. Belatedly, Great Britain now began an extensive reorganization of her overseas dominions. The American colonies took violent exception to the measures adopted by King and Parliament, until, in 1775, peaceable discussion was replaced by open warfare. Yet even after armed conflict broke out, the colonists continued to protest their loyalty, affirming that they sought only to maintain their rights against unconstitutional measures of the home government. The logic of events, however, presently compelled them to recognize that they had embarked upon a Revolutionary War, actually a struggle for separate political life. This fact was finally advertised to the world in the Declaration of Independence, adopted July 4, 1776.

Following the Battle of Bunker Hill (June 17, 1775), thousands of eager "minute men" swarmed to Boston, where, despite being undisciplined and poorly equipped, they penned the British troops under General Gage within the city. Volumes have been written about the Battle of Bunker Hill, but we have no real knowledge that any American flag was flown in it. John Trumbull, whose paintings of Revolutionary War scenes are widely famous, was an eye-witness, and his subsequent drawing depicting the battle, with the Americans giving way before the final British assault, shows two flags prominently displayed. One of these was a red flag having a green tree on a white union in the first canton, the other a red flag of solid color with no discernible design. A variant of the former, but with a blue field and a red cross in the white union, is also credited by tradition (Pl. II-6). Although Trumbull took great pains to obtain correct representations of his human subjects, he gave free rein to artistic fancy in other respects. He cannot be depended upon, therefore, in regard to all details.[3]

On July 3, 1775, at Cambridge, just outside Boston, George Washington assumed general command of all the American forces and began the arduous task of transforming them into a real army. No thought had been given to a common flag for this army, although the many companies and regiments which composed it brought to the field a wide variety of banners. Most of these have long since vanished, but a few remain and we have reliable information concerning a number of others. Eight such flags are pictured in this book (Pl. II-7, 8, 9; Pl. III-10, 11, 12, 13, 14).[4]

In September, 1775, two floating batteries were launched on the Charles River to harass the defenders of Boston, and about the same time preparation of a fleet of armed schooners was begun. On October 20 Colonel Joseph Reed, Washington's military secretary, wrote to the agents engaged in outfitting these ships: "Please fix upon some particular color for a flag and a signal by which our vessels may know one another. What do you think of a flag with a white ground and a tree in the middle with the motto 'An Appeal to Heaven'? This is the flag of our floating batteries." During the next few months a fleet of several vessels put to sea under the Green Tree Flag which Reed had suggested. But leaving such a matter for an Army contractor to decide shows how little attention either General Washington or the members of Congress had yet given to the subject of a common flag.

There is further indication of this. A committee of Congress visited the Army in October to confer with Washington and others upon "the most effective method of continuing, supporting, and regulating a Continental Army." Its detailed report, rendered to Congress on November 2, 1775, was thoroughly discussed and several resolutions were adopted fixing the size of the new Army, troop rations and pay, and other pertinent details. These enactments supplied the legal basis for organization of our first national military establishment. Again, however, if any thought was given to designing a flag for the new Army, the records are entirely silent concerning it.

Washington's task of organizing the Continental Army progressed so rapidly that on January 1, 1776, it came into formal existence. By way of celebrating this event—in effect the birthday of America's national Army—the Commander in Chief issued a general pardon to all military offenders. Of more lasting interest was a ceremony staged on Prospect Hill, in Somerville, where a seventy-six-foot flagstaff had been erected, so lofty that it could be seen even in distant Boston. On this was hoisted the "Union Flag in Compliment to the United Colonies."[5]

This Great or Grand Union Flag was nothing more than the Meteor Flag of Great Britain modified by having six horizontal white stripes imposed on its field, thereby dividing the field into thirteen alternate red and white stripes (Pl. IV-15). These of course signified the thirteen original colonies, while retention of the British Union in the first canton testified continued loyalty, as Americans saw it, to the constitution of the government against which they fought. By strange coincidence, if not indeed design, the Great Union was remarkably like the flag of the British East India Company, 1707-1858 (Pl. IV-16), which was probably known to at least some Americans, especially the seafarers of New England.

Three days after the Prospect Hill ceremony, on January 4, 1776, the new fleet at Philadelphia, which Congress had entrusted to the command of Esek Hopkins, of Rhode Island, put to sea. On March 17 these ships captured the town of New Providence in the Bahama Islands, with about one hundred cannon and extensive military stores of other kinds. In this first salt-water baptism of the American Navy its vessels flew the Great Union Flag.

Hopkins's cruise is also notable for another reason. Congress had authorized the organization of two companies of Marines, which went on the voyage. This marks the birth of the United States Marine Corps. In a letter of December 27, 1775, a contemporary observer records that on one of the Marines' drums a rattlesnake was painted with the motto "Don't tread on me" beneath it.[6] Two additional flags carried by the fleet were Commodore Hopkins's Broad Pennant, a yellow flag having upon it a coiled rattlesnake about to strike, and a "striped Jack" which probably consisted of thirteen alternate red and white stripes with a serpent stretched diagonally across its field (Pl. V-17). This flag, sometimes without the serpent, was in common use for many years, particularly at sea, and was known as the American Stripes (Pl. V-18).[7] Another interesting flag of similar design, but with seven red and six blue stripes crossed diagonally by the serpent, and with the motto "Don't Tread on Me" at the top, was used by the naval forces of South Carolina in the Revolutionary War (Pl. V-19).

From January 1, 1776, on, therefore, the colonists had in the Great Union Flag a symbol expressive of their unity, adopted for use in the Navy and over fortifications ashore, although not generally used as a land battle flag. While Congress never formally adopted it, this banner soon became known as the "Union Flag," the "Grand Union Flag," the "Congress Flag," and the "Colours of the United Colonies." By April, 1776, an excellent representation of it was shown on the paper currency of North Carolina.[8] When the American Army occupied New York that year, following the British evacuation of Boston, the Great Union Flag was hoisted over the fort at the lower end of Manhattan Island.[9] And on Lake Champlain in the summer of 1776 Benedict Arnold flew it over his tiny fleet, which was crushed in the desperate Battle of Valcour Island, October 11-12 following.

By that time, however, the Great Union Flag was already obsolete. The Declaration of Independence had removed the last possibility of reconciliation with the mother country. Henceforth the colonists openly recognized themselves as revolutionists, fighting for national independence. The Great Union Flag, with its crosses of St. George and St. Andrew, symbolizing loyalty to the Crown, no longer answered their needs. As time passed it fell more and more into disuse. On land, the last action in which it seems to have figured was the siege of Fort Schuyler in August, 1777. Although its period of usefulness was short, it nevertheless played an important role in our history. The Great Union banner was the first United States national flag, and from it, by one simple change, the Stars and Stripes was created.

CHAPTER 2 ★

A New Constellation

CONGRESS CONVENED AT PHILADELPHIA ON JUNE 14, 1777, to spend the day upon an accumulation of routine matters. General Burgoyne was launching a new invasion of the colonies from Canada by way of Lake Champlain, which Carleton had weakly abandoned in 1776. Progress of the Revolutionary War to date gave scant cause for its leaders to view the future with optimism. Yet life must go on, and so Congress resumed the unceasing struggle to cope with its many problems. Its journal for that day records formal proceedings, but preserves nothing of the discussions which attended them.

Two orders for the payment of money to Mr. John Murray were passed. A letter of May 20 from Amos Throop, of Providence, was read and referred to the Marine Committee. Varying sums of money were then appropriated for the use of several independent militia companies, after which the Marine Committee was authorized to dispose of the ships of the Continental Navy in the Delaware should the enemy succeed in their impending attempt upon the "said river."

Next in the journal of Congress for that day came a short but momentous one-sentence entry: "RESOLVED: that the flag of the United States be made of thirteen stripes, alternate red and white; that the union be thirteen stars, white in a blue field, representing a new constellation." A communication from the State of Massachusetts Bay, asserting that Captain John Roach (who had been appointed commander of the *Ranger,* another ship in the Continental Navy) was a person of doubtful character, having next been read, the gentleman was suspended until an inquiry into his conduct could be made. John Paul Jones was given the vacant command. Finally, with these and a number of other matters disposed of, Congress "Adjourned to 10 o'clock on Monday."

Thus was the charter of the Stars and Stripes enacted in one brief resolution, unattended by even a single word of introduction or explanation. The reason for the change, however, seems clear enough. Although Congress had never formally adopted the Great Union Flag, its members knew about it, and in all probability they now acted in the light of this knowledge. That banner had been created by adding six white stripes to the field of England's red Meteor Flag. Now Congress merely removed the obnoxious crosses of St. George and St. Andrew from the first canton and replaced them with "thirteen stars, white in a blue field, representing a new constellation." Union of the thirteen colonies was thereby doubly signified: once by the thirteen red and white stripes of the Great Union Flag, and again by the thirteen stars now added to it. Slight as this change was, it expressed a tremendous fact symbolically, advertising to the world the resolution formally voted by Congress almost a year earlier "that these United Colonies are, and of Right ought to be, Free and Independent States."

Another consideration, clearly apparent in the resolution of June 14, demands our attention. This gives no detailed description of the new flag, and until some authority provided one, every seamstress who might undertake to make such a banner would naturally feel free to follow her own fancy, if not that of her employer, in designing it. Such questions as the proportions of the flag, the size of the union or canton, and the design and arrangement of the stars on their blue field were all left hanging in the air. Nor were these questions officially answered for almost a century and a half after 1777, thus affording room for widely varying interpretation of details in the design of the Stars and Stripes, especially with regard to the stars. It is possible that the vertical stripes in our Customs Flag may also have derived from the whim of some early flag maker.[1]

Still another important consideration concerns the use which Congress intended should be made of the flag. It will be recalled that the Flag Resolution of June 14, 1777, was preceded and followed by other actions dealing with routine naval activities referred to Congress by its Marine Committee. As was the custom of Great Britain, from which so much of American procedure follows, the Great Union Flag had been used at sea and over fixed fortresses on land. In like manner its successor, the Stars and Stripes, seems to have been designed for use as a marine flag, not for a battle flag on land.

PLATE III

10
Rhode Island Revolutionary War Flag

11
Flag of the Green Mountain Boys, Revolutionary War

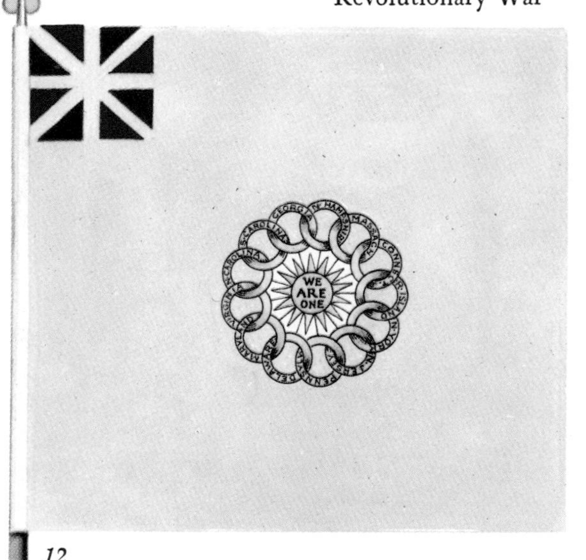

12
Flag of the 2nd New Hampshire Regiment, Revolutionary War

13
Gadsden or South Carolina Rattlesnake Flag, Revolutionary War

14
New England Pine Tree Flag ("An Appeal to Heaven"), the flag of Washington's Cruisers, Revolutionary War

Plate IV

15
Great or Grand Union Flag, Revolutionary War, raised over Continental Army at Cambridge, Mass., January, 1776. This flag continued to be used after the Stars and Stripes flag was authorized by the Continental Congress.

16
Flag of the British East India Company, 1707-1858. It apparently was the parent of the Grand Union Flag.

Although the resolution creating the flag was adopted on June 14, weeks passed before it was noticed in the press. Finally it was printed on September 2, 1777, in *Dunlap's Pennsylvania Packet, or the General Advertiser,* in a column reporting various proceedings of Congress. By the middle of that month, news of the resolution had been carried to Boston, where it was published in the Boston *Gazette* on the 15th and in the Massachusetts *Spy* three days later.

In this simple chronology lies the refutation of many statements found in books dealing with the history of the flag concerning early use of the Stars and Stripes in land battles of the Revolutionary War. "The starry banner was displayed," says one writer, "at the battle of Brandywine on September 11, at Germantown on the 4th of October, and when Burgoyne surrendered at Saratoga, on the 17th of that month, and thenceforward during all the battles of the Revolution."[2] Such sweeping claims are unsupported by the evidence, as discussed in Chapter 5 of this book. The fact is that to the very end of the Revolutionary War the Stars and Stripes was neither officially supplied to the Continental Army by Congress, nor does it appear ever to have been intended for use in land engagements.

On February 20, 1776, an order was issued permitting colonels of American regiments and certain others "to fix upon any such [colors] as they could procure and might deem proper." This was more than a year before adoption of the Flag Resolution of June 14, 1777, and it indicates that neither General Washington nor Congress had given consideration to using the Great Union Flag in land battles. Indeed, it was more than three years after that resolution was passed that the Commander in Chief and the Board of War took up, as if for the first time, the question of what design the Continental Army flags should have.

Richard Peters, Secretary of the Board, wrote to Washington on May 10, 1779:

The Board have been frequently applied to on the Subject of Drums and Colours for the several Regiments. It is impossible to comply with all the Requisitions for these Articles as we have not materials to make either in sufficient numbers. We hope however to have in a short Time a competent Number of Drums . . . as to Colours, we have refused them for another Reason. The Baron Steuben mentioned when he was here that he would settle with your Excellency some Plan as to the Colours. It was intended that every Regiment should have two Colours—one the Standard of the United States, which should be the same throughout the Army, and the other a Regimental Colour which should vary according to the facings of the Regiment. *But it is not yet settled what is the Standard of the U. States.* If your Excellency will therefore favour us with your Opinion on the Subject we will report to Congress and request them to establish a Standard and so soon as this is done we will endeavour to get Materials and order a Number made sufficient for the Army. Neither can we tell what should be the Regimental Colours as Uniforms were by a late Resolution of Congress to be settled by Your Excellency.[3]

So we see that almost two years after the Flag Resolution of June 14, 1777, Congress had neither supplied the Continental Army with flags nor had it even decided on their design. As in the armies of England and France, however, each regiment was to carry two colors, one its own regimental flag, the other the national standard. And since the letter quoted indicates that the "Standard of the U. States" had not yet been settled upon, it seems clear that this was not intended to be the Stars and Stripes.

On May 14, 1779, Washington replied to the Board of War that "the arrangement respecting Colours" had not yet been made. Nor was there any decision on this point up to September 3 following, when we find Secretary Peters sending the General drafts of an army standard for his "Approbation, Rejection, or Alteration." His letter added: "The one with the Union and Emblem in the middle is preferred by us as being variant from the Marine Flag."

This "Marine Flag," it can safely be assumed, was the Stars and Stripes, and Peters's letter discloses that the Board of War desired an entirely different banner for the Continental Army. Replying on September 14, Washington agreed with the board in favoring a standard having "the Union and Emblem in the middle," but he further stated that the regimental number and the name of the State to which it belonged ought to be inserted "within the curve of the serpent." Unfortunately, no copy of the proposed design has been preserved, and we have no definite knowledge of what it was. The seal adopted by the War Office in 1778, and still in use, shows two flags, one the Stars and Stripes with a rectangular arrangement of the stars on the field of the union, the other (apparently a regimental flag) plain and without design of any kind. Above is a curved rattlesnake with the motto "This We'll Defend," surrounded by its folds. It is a matter of speculation whether this seal reproduces the flag design which Washington and the Board of War were discussing.

In any event, nothing came of this exchange of ideas, for late in

February, 1780, in response to Washington's complaint of a "great deficiency" of drums, fifes, and standards, Peters replied:

> As many Colours as possible shall be provided, but until we receive the Articles from France . . . we cannot have the Standards prepared agreeably to the Plan Proposed, viz. to have two for every Regt—one the Standard of the United States, the other the Regimental Standard, the Ground whereof to be the Colour of the Facing. The Regiments must shift with what Colours can now be given them until the arrival of our expected supplies.

Washington answered this communication on March 6, 1780, expressing his "great pleasure" over the prospect of receiving the promised supplies. But he was doomed to still further disappointment. More than two years later, on August 6, 1782, we find him writing from Newburgh that he "could wish" the colors might be sent to him soon, having been informed that they were already purchased.

"The colours are ready and will be immediately sent—as also the drums and fifes as fast as they can be obtained," General Lincoln wrote hopefully for the Board of War on August 8. Seven months later, on March 1, 1783, the patient Commander in Chief was finally told by the board that "the Standards are in the hands of the Quarter Master . . . and have been there for some time." So the flags had come at last! Replying on March 11, Washington stated that he had in fact found the standards in possession of the military storekeeper, but noted that Lincoln's letter of March 1 afforded him the first notice that they were near him.

Ironically, the flags were no longer needed. The Revolutionary War had ended, for all practical purposes, a year and a half earlier at Yorktown. And to complete this story of frustration, we have no record either of what was done with these long-sought standards or of the design or designs they bore.

PLATE VI

21
Flags flown by the American ships *Alliance* and *Serapis* in 1779. These paintings were made by a Dutch artist in the port of Texel, Holland. The top flag, painted October 4, 1779, flew on the *Alliance*. The bottom flag, painted October 5, 1779, flew on the *Serapis,* John Paul Jones's prize ship, taken from the British in one of the most desperate sea fights of the Revolutionary War. Commodore Byron McCandless, U.S.N., in December 1923, discovered the paintings of these flags in the Gunther collection, then uncatalogued, at the Chicago Historical Society. The original paintings are now in that society. *Courtesy Chicago Historical Society*

conscious, the mythmakers were thus left wholly free to exercise their fancy upon the subject.

One claimant for honor, however, stands in a class by himself, and is to some extent an exception to the above statements. Francis Hopkinson was a man of culture and ability, an ardent advocate of independence, who had been for a time a member of Congress from New Jersey. A few months after adoption of the Flag Resolution he was appointed one of the three Commissioners of the Continental Navy Board, to which had been entrusted the administration of American naval affairs. As chairman and secretary of this board, Hopkinson served capably for almost two years. Then he became Treasurer of Loans, to which office Congress had elected him. A year later, while still serving in that capacity, he took over the important post of Judge of the Pennsylvania Admiralty Court.[2]

Hopkinson possessed both poetic and artistic ability, and at various times he designed, or assisted in designing, seals of the American Philosophical Society, the State of New Jersey, and the College of Philadelphia, predecessor of the University of Pennsylvania. He had been closely associated with naval matters when the Flag Resolution of June 14, 1777, was adopted by Congress, and on May 25, 1780, he addressed a letter to the Board of Admiralty expressing pleasure that his device of a seal for that board had met with approval. The same letter requested recognition for this work and a number of similar services he had from time to time performed. "I have with great Readiness," he continued, "upon several Occasions exerted my small abilities in this Way for the public service, as I flatter myself, to the satisfaction of those I wished to please." This statement was followed by a list of the "devices" he had created, beginning with "the Flag of the United States of America," and including seals for the Admiralty, the Treasury Board, and the Great Seal of the United States, besides a variety of work on the Continental currency. For all this work he had made no charge, and he now asked the board whether a quarter cask of the public wine would not be deemed a proper reward "for these Labours of Fancy."

Hopkinson's request was referred to Congress, and in the course of ensuing prolonged discussion he was led to submit several restatements of his services, on which he now placed a value of £2,700 in currency, or £45 in "hard money." Incidental to these several restatements he successively characterized the flag he had designed (for which particular item he asked £9 cash or £540 in paper money) as "the Flag of the United States of America," "the great Naval Flag of the United States" and "the Naval Flag of the States." Although the Treasury authorities at first favored his claim for compensation, in the end it was rejected. Hopkinson charged the Treasury Board with misconduct and a serious quarrel ensued, the upshot of which was his resignation as Treasurer of Loans. Finally, as the result of an investigation by a committee of Congress, which stated that he was not the only person who had worked on designs for the flag, that body resolved on August 23, 1781, "that the report relative to the fancy-work of F. Hopkinson ought not to be acted upon."

The conclusion drawn from all this by Hopkinson's biographer seems amply justified: that within three years after adoption of the Flag Resolution, repeated assertions were made by Hopkinson in writing, to men who had ready means of knowing the truth of the matter, that he had designed the Stars and Stripes; nor did his enemies on the Treasury Board deny the claim. Accepting such conclusion as valid, however, what does it signify? Nothing more, apparently, than that Hopkinson had prepared a drawing, for which he demanded £9 cash payment. Was the idea for design of the flag his own suggestion, or did someone else originally conceive the thought of replacing the crosses of St. George and St. Andrew in the canton with thirteen stars on a blue field "representing a new constellation"? This question still remains unanswered, nor do we have any information to prove that practical use was made of Hopkinson's sketch. Congress did not proceed to supply the Continental Army with flags, nor did it furnish them for the American Navy. The few existing or recorded Revolutionary War flags with stars and stripes vary widely from one another in detail. The design most often attributed to Hopkinson is that of a banner having seven red and six white stripes, and with thirteen five-pointed white stars arranged in a 3-2-3-2-3 order on the blue union (Pl. V-20). It is impossible to say, however, what his "device" was really like, or if any flag of that precise description was ever flown in the Revolutionary War.

CHAPTER 4 ★

The Stars Afloat

IN 1778 THE KING OF NAPLES DECIDED TO OPEN HIS ports to American ships, and that October his ambassador at the French Court asked Benjamin Franklin and John Adams, the American Commissioners there, to furnish him with a description of their flag.

"It is with pleasure," they replied, "that we acquaint your Excellency that the flag of the United States of America consists of 13 stripes, alternately red, white and blue; a small square in the upper angle, next the flag staff, is a blue field, with 13 white stars, denoting a new Constellation."

"Some of the States," continued the Commissioners, "have vessels of war distinct from those of the United States. For example, the vessels of war of the State of Massachusetts Bay have sometimes a pine tree; and those of South Carolina a rattlesnake in the middle of the 13 stripes; but the flag of the United States, ordained by Congress, is the 13 stripes and 13 stars above described."[1]

On sea as on land, therefore, a wide variety of American flags was displayed, and almost a year and a half after the birth of the Stars and Stripes the two foremost American spokesmen in Europe could describe it in an official communication as having "red, white and blue" stripes. Their seeming error is significant, for it is inconceivable that Franklin or Adams could possibly have been ignorant of the descriptive language in the Flag Resolution of June 14, 1777.

No sailors in the world excelled American seamen of the Revolutionary War period. Hardly had the conflict begun when scores of ships, privately owned or manned, put to sea to prey on British commerce. Massachusetts alone sent out more than sixteen hundred privateersmen, chiefly during the war's earlier years. Sailing under a great variety of flags, they brought terror and destruction to Britain's far-flung ocean trade, and presently it became a matter of concern to neutral European governments how to identify the country to which they claimed allegiance. Upon this scene of confusion appeared John Paul Jones in the sloop *Ranger,* flying the brand-new Stars and Stripes. To him belongs the distinction of being the first to obtain foreign recognition for the flag, and also the first to baptize it, victoriously, in battle.

Jones, as we have seen in a previous chapter, had been appointed by Congress to command the *Ranger* on the same day that the Flag Resolution was adopted. Following several months devoted to outfitting his ship, he sailed for France early in November, 1777, commissioned by Congress to convey the news of Burgoyne's surrender in mid-October to our representatives in Paris.

No Hollywood press agent ever advertised his client more successfully than did Jones the Stars and Stripes to the governments of Europe. On February 14, 1778, he induced the Admiral of the French Fleet in Quiberon Bay to exchange salutes with his vessel, thereby gaining the first formal recognition of the American Flag by a foreign power. Two months later he sailed from Brest for a descent upon the English coast, and in an hour-long battle on April 24 defeated the British sloop *Drake,* whose surrender saw "The American Stars," hoisted during the struggle, float for the first time triumphant over a beaten foe.[2]

After long delay, the French Government supplied Jones with a fleet of several small vessels. With these, in mid-August, 1779, he sailed for a second descent upon British home waters. His flagship was an over-age French vessel, which by way of a compliment to Benjamin Franklin and his *Poor Richard's Almanack* he renamed the *Bon Homme Richard.* Other ships of the little fleet, which it was agreed should sail under the Stars and Stripes, included the *Alliance* and the *Pallas.*

On September 23, 1779, after rounding Ireland and Scotland, Jones fell in with a large number of merchantmen, convoyed by the forty-gun British frigate *Serapis* and the smaller *Countess of Scarborough.* The *Pallas* engaged and captured the latter vessel, while Jones in the *Bon Homme Richard* made for the *Serapis,* whose armament was so superior that his only hope of success lay in coming to close quarters with the enemy.

Jones managed to lash the *Richard* to the *Serapis.* Then the two ships fought, muzzle to muzzle, for over three hours, in a desperate naval battle. The *Richard* was presently so damaged that only by the use of her pumps could she be kept from sinking. At length her gunner, thinking that all was lost, rushed to the poop deck to strike the flag, and finding it had been carried away by a cannon shot he called out for quarter. Upon this, Captain Pearson of the *Serapis* demanded to know whether the American ship had surrendered; to which Jones himself, opportunely appearing on the scene, answered something to the effect that he had "not yet begun to fight." Such at least is the version of his words which has become hallowed by tradition, though Jones himself merely stated, in his report on the battle made to Benjamin Franklin shortly afterward, that he had replied "in the most determined negative."[3]

American resolution finally overcame British doggedness and Captain Pearson struck his flag. Because of the sinking condition of the *Bon Homme Richard,* Jones transferred his crew to the *Serapis* and with his squadron sailed for Holland. En route, the *Richard* sank on the second day after the battle. The remaining vessels reached Texel, an island off the Dutch coast, on October 3. The British Ambassador at The Hague promptly demanded that the Dutch Government seize Jones's ships and their crews, charging that the American captain was a criminal and a pirate, sailing under the flag of no recognized nation.

From this demand proceeded one of the most notable episodes in the history of the Stars and Stripes. The prudent Dutch dispatched an artist to make a careful drawing of the flags which the American vessels displayed. Fortunately for our knowledge of the subject, the industrious artist drew two pictures, one showing the flag of the *Alliance,* the other that of the *Serapis,* now Jones's flagship. Both were painted in color, and they constitute our earliest actual representations of the Stars and Stripes as first displayed at sea. Now preserved at the Chicago Historical Society, the paintings are reproduced in this book through the courtesy of that institution (Pl. VI-21).[4]

Several significant conclusions emerge from an inspection of these pictures. The two flags differ from each other in numerous respects. The fly or length of the *Alliance* flag is considerably longer than its width on the staff. It has seven white and six red stripes, and seven stripes extend beneath the union. The thirteen white stars in the blue field of the union, eight-pointed and crudely made, are arranged in 3-2-3-2-3 order.

The fly of the *Serapis*'s flag, on the other hand, is but little longer than its width on the staff. The union is smaller, having eight of the thirteen stripes below it. Its eight-pointed white stars in the blue field of the union are arranged in three horizontal rows of four, five, and four. More surprising than these details, however, are the thirteen stripes: red, white, and blue, just as Franklin and Adams had reported to the Neapolitan ambassador (four white, four blue, and five red). Nor are the colors arranged in regular order. The top stripe is blue and the lowest one is red, but the flag maker followed no orderly sequence of rotating the colors between these two. One of the stars has seven points instead of eight, but all are so crudely made that this variation seems to have no particular importance.

So we see that the seamtresses (or artists, in the case of painted flags) who fashioned the early Stars and Stripes apparently followed their own individual ideas with respect to much of the design. Nor could they do otherwise, if they were to make a flag at all, the provisions of the Flag Resolution of June 14, 1777, being so general that flag makers necessarily had to fill in details as their personal fancy or artistic imagination dictated. Eighteenth-century Americans were practical men who utilized a flag for the purpose of identifying their national allegiance. This accomplished, they wasted neither time nor sentiment on precise details of design. That John Paul Jones, who was undoubtedly familiar with provisions of the Flag Resolution, should use the *Serapis*'s flag with its blue stripes, affords proof of this attitude. As a matter of sober fact, it was not until 1912, some 135 years after the birth of the Stars and Stripes, that the Federal Government really bothered to prescribe exactly how our national flag should look.

Variation in the design of flags made in the Revolutionary War period was likewise promoted by an apparent lack of published descriptions of the Stars and Stripes. A flag sheet published in 1780 by Mondhare, in Paris, is the earliest printed depiction known to scholars. A second copy of this same plate, but dated 1781, is in the John Carter Brown Library at Providence, Rhode Island, and is illustrated in connection with the present narrative (Pl. VII-22). Among a series of colored drawings of flags borne by ships throughout the world, it shows two United States naval banners, one the flag of American merchantmen, the other the flag of the American Congress

—the Stars and Stripes. The mercantile flag is the familiar red and white American stripes. The Congress flag has seven red and six white horizontal stripes, with eleven of them extending only to the blue field of the union. On the latter, twelve white stars are arranged in four horizontal rows of three stars each. Above these, apparently as a substitute for the thirteenth star, is a French *fleur-de-lis.*[5] Also shown (Pl. VII-23) are two United States naval pennants. One of these has two broad stripes, red on top and white at the bottom. The other has a blue union next to the staff with three rows of four stars each, and the same curious *fleur-de-lis* serving as the thirteenth star just at the left of the top row. To the right of the union is a series of vertical red and white stripes, beginning with red, of which only six stripes are visible as the pennant is furled. The pennant ends in a tapered point with two large horizontal stripes, red above white.

Also of interest in this connection is Mathieu Alber and George F. Lotter, *Tableau de Tous les Pavillons que l'on Arbore sur les Vaisseaux dans les Quatre Parties du Monde* . . . (Augsburg: 1793), a copy of which is in The Mariners Museum at Newport News, Virginia. Three American marine flags are pictured in this book, and all are here reproduced. One of them, labeled "P. du Congress Americain," has thirteen six-pointed white stars in a blue union next the staff, arranged in rows of 3-2-3-2-3; and in its field are thirteen stripes, starting at the top, red, blue, and white, in that order of alternation, with the bottom stripe being red (Pl. VIII-24). The second flag, labeled "P. March.[d] des Etats unis de l'Amerique," has thirteen stripes of red, blue, and white, starting at the top, followed by one red stripe at the bottom, with no blue field or stars (Pl. VIII-25). And the third flag in this series, labeled "Autres Flamme des Etats unis de l'Amerique," is really a pennant. It has a blue union with thirteen six-pointed white stars arranged in rows of 3-2-3-2-3; immediately to the right of this thirteen *vertical* stripes of red, blue, and white in series order, the thirteenth stripe being red; and to the right of these three horizontal stripes of red, blue, and white, with the red stripe at the top. The tapered ends of this pennant have a red stripe at the top and a white stripe at the bottom, the blue stripe being cut out (Pl. IX-26).

Whether the illustrations thus described were made from examination of actual American flags, and if so how accurate they were, must remain unsettled questions for the moment. Be that as it may, they do serve to indicate further that, far from being uniform in design, the early Stars and Stripes exhibited marked variation in both color and arrangement of component details.

It is characteristic of Americans to imagine that each war in which they have engaged will be the last one, and at its conclusion to dismantle their military and naval establishments. So it was at the close of the Revolutionary War. The *Alliance,* the last remaining United States warship, was sold in August, 1785. Thenceforth, until a new navy was established in 1794, only American merchant ships carried the flag over alien seas and into foreign harbors.

By his exploits John Paul Jones had advertised the Stars and Stripes well to the nations of western Europe. It remained for another renowned seaman, a decade later, to introduce it to oriental waters. That story begins when final outcome of the Revolutionary War was much in doubt.

On July 4, 1776, in London, Captain James Cook received instructions to sail in search of the "Northwest Passage" around North America. Although he failed to find such a route, Cook made extensive surveys from 1776 to 1779, when he was killed in the Sandwich (Hawaiian) Islands. From these surveys the European world gained its first real knowledge of the western American coast from California to Cape Prince of Wales.

Two incidental consequences of interest here resulted from Cook's last voyage. Along the northwest coast of America crowds of natives visited his ships eager to trade for the white man's goods, offering in exchange sea otter skins and other furs which the sailors were glad to obtain for use as clothing and bedding. When the Englishmen later arrived at Canton, however, they were amazed to find that the Chinese merchants were willing to pay fabulous prices for their furs. Skins which had been obtained for a few pennies' value in America sold there readily for $100 or more.

Minus their dead captain, Cook's vessel finally returned to Holland in October, 1780, bringing news of their discoveries on the four-year voyage. Among the sailors who had taken part was a Connecticut Yankee named John Ledyard. He subsequently returned to America, published an account of the trip in 1783, and at about the same time tried to induce Boston and New York merchants to organize an expedition to the Northwest Coast and China to exploit the commercial opportunity which Cook's crews had stumbled upon.[6]

Although Ledyard failed to accomplish his objective, the project he had envisioned was presently taken up by others. Thus in 1787 a group of Boston merchants outfitted two small vessels, the *Columbia* and the *Lady Washington,* to venture the new route around Cape Horn and across the Pacific. Flying the American Flag, they sailed from Boston on September 30, 1787, and a year later reached the coast of what is now British Columbia. There both ships passed the winter of 1788-89. Then, on July 30, 1789, having collected a quantity of sea otter skins along the coast, Captain Robert Gray sailed for China in the *Columbia.* Arriving at Canton, he remained there about three months, exchanging his furs for a cargo of tea. Finally the *Columbia* turned her prow homeward, and on August 6, 1790, Gray cast anchor once more in Boston Harbor. The memorable voyage had covered 42,000 miles, and with it the Stars and Stripes was for the first time carried around the world.[7]

CHAPTER 5 ★

First Honors on Land

ALTHOUGH THE "STANDARD OF THE UNITED STATES" was not officially supplied to the Continental Army by Congress until 1783, this does not mean that the Stars and Stripes could not have been flown, somewhere or other, perhaps even in many places, during the Revolutionary War. Actually, various claims have been advanced, with different degrees of support, that it was.

The statement that Washington first displayed the Stars and Stripes at Assunpink, near Trenton, New Jersey, cannot be regarded seriously, competent students being in agreement that no flag of this type was raised anywhere until sometime after June 14, 1777. Similarly with the claim that such a flag was flown by the American Commander in Chief at Middlebrook, near Bound Brook in the same State, beginning on June 15, 1777. "The inherent improbability of this story," says the historian John Spargo, "is so great that its acceptance as anything more than an ingenious legend requires a much greater weight of critically tested evidence than has yet been adduced in its support. Indeed, not a shred of actual evidence has been cited in proof of the claim, only abstract argument and ingenious references."[1]

Nor is there any positive proof, as has sometimes been stated, that the Stars and Stripes was hoisted at the Battle of Hubbardton, in Vermont, on July 7, 1777.[2] Two days later, however, at Fort Anne, New York, the opposing forces met in another engagement. In that action, as a British officer recorded in his journal on July 10, "the 9th took their colours, which were intended as a present to their Colonel Lord Ligonier. They were very handsome, a flag of the United States, 13 stripes alternate red and white, [with thirteen stars] in a blue field representing a new constellation."[3] The bracketed phrase seems to have been an insertion by the editor of this journal, James Phineas Baxter, who apparently worked from a copy which he found in the British Museum, but the language immediately following obviously harks back to the Flag Resolution adopted by Congress on June 14 preceding.

Much more forcibly advanced is the oft-repeated claim about the American banner flown at Fort Schuyler (Stanwix), in New York State, during the siege of its works by Colonel Barry St. Leger in the summer of 1777. Spargo made an exhaustive study of this assertion, too, coming to the well-documented conclusion that the flag in question "was not the Stars and Stripes, but a flag of the same design as that raised by Washington at Cambridge on taking command of the Continental Army, having thirteen alternating red and white stripes and the united crosses of St. George and St. Andrew in the canton."[4] Not least interesting in this connection is a decorated powder horn facing page 27 of Spargo's book. The horn was engraved by Private John McGraw and is dated December 25, 1777 (Pl. X-28). It shows a flag flying over the works which, while the cross of St. George is missing, was obviously meant to be the Great Union banner first flown at Cambridge.

What is believed by some to be the oldest Stars and Stripes now in existence is the so-called Bennington Flag, supposed to have been used by the Bennington militia at the Battle of Bennington, just over the Vermont border, in New York State, August 16, 1777, and now in possession of the Bennington Battle Monument and Historical Association, Bennington, Vermont. No contemporary records can be cited in proof, but a long-standing tradition asserts that this flag was raised at Bennington by Nathaniel Fillmore, grandfather of President Fillmore, who kept it until the War of 1812, when he gave it to his nephew, Septa Fillmore. Thence the old banner passed on to other members of the Fillmore family down through the years, being exhibited for a time in the G.A.R. Room of the Chicago Public Library, until Mrs. Henry G. Wilson, the last Fillmore owner, presented it as a gift to the Association in 1926. Spargo makes a good case for the Revolutionary War authenticity of this flag.[5]

The Bennington Flag is illustrated on Plate IX-27. Its design is unique in some ways, and introduces at least one element not mentioned in the Flag Resolution of June 14, 1777. There are seven white and six red stripes, and only four stripes below the lower edge of the canton. The blue union has thirteen seven-pointed white stars, eleven of which form an arch surrounding the numeral "76," which is also in white. The other two stars are located one in each upper corner of the union or canton, above this arch. The Bennington Flag is also quite large, measuring ten feet long by five and one-half feet wide, seemingly too unwieldy to have been carried in the midst of battle. Every portion of it is hand-spun, hand-woven, and hand-sewn linen.[6]

Assertions have also been made that the Stars and Stripes was in evidence at the Battle of Cooch's Bridge, in Delaware, September 3, 1777; and the historian Preble says that the national flag was undoubtedly unfurled at the Battle of Brandywine, in Pennsylvania, on September 11 of the same year, only eight days after its official promulgation at Philadelphia. Neither case, of course, is outside the realm of possibility, but no real documentation for these two claims has ever been forthcoming.[7]

Many historians believe that the Stars and Stripes was raised at Burgoyne's surrender, on October 17, 1777, following British defeat at the Battle of Saratoga. Trumbull's well-known painting of that memorable event, in the Capitol at Washington, D.C., shows such a flag waving over the tent of the American commander, General Horatio Gates. In this instance there are seven red and six white stripes. Twelve six-pointed white stars are arranged in the form of a square in the blue union, with the thirteenth star in the center.[8] Trumbull was not present at the Battle of Saratoga, however, and did not execute his picture of Burgoyne's surrender until many years afterward. Also, his painting of the Battle of Princeton, January 3, 1777, depicts a similar Stars and Stripes, which could hardly have existed at that time.

The most that can be said for Saratoga, therefore, is that a Stars and Stripes in some form or other, possibly even the Bennington Flag, was used. Even this is only theoretical, or at best a matter of probability, as no positive proof has yet come to light.[9]

Still another claimant for Stars and Stripes honors is the flag said to have been carried by the North Carolina militiamen at the Battle of Guilford Courthouse, March 15, 1781 (Pl. XI-29). Now preserved in the North Carolina Hall of History, at Raleigh, this is the only one which R. C. Ballard Thruston, a noted flag authority, feels confident was actually borne by American troops in the Revolutionary War. It is nearly three times as long as wide, and has seven blue and six red stripes. Against the white ground of the union are thirteen eight-pointed blue stars of unusually large size, arranged in rows of four, three, and four, with the twelfth and thirteenth additional stars to the right of these, somewhat midpoint between the rows.[10] Although this flag approximates the general design of that prescribed by Congress on June 14, 1777, its color details do not conform with the language of the Flag Resolution.

In great contrast to the Guilford Courthouse banner is another flag, supposed to have been used by the Third Maryland Regiment at the Battle of Cowpens, in South Carolina, January 17, 1781 (Pl. XI-30). The details of this are so completely in accord with the general phraseology of the Flag Resolution as to raise a question whether it actually dates back to the Revolutionary War. Here there are seven red and six white stripes; the flag is but twice as long as wide; the union extends but one-third the length of the fly, and in depth through but seven of the thirteen stripes; and twelve five-pointed white stars of conventional size are arranged in a circle on the blue ground of the union, with the thirteenth star in the center.[11] Regardless of the claims made for it, this flag was a regimental standard, not necessarily a national banner.

Still another early Stars and Stripes is the flag which is supposed to have floated over Fort Independence, at Boston, in 1781 (Pl. XII-31). On this the stars are arranged in rows of 4-5-4, making the appropriate total of thirteen.[12] Little is known about it, but it must be classed as a garrison, rather than a battle flag.

Finally there is the case of Yorktown, where Cornwallis surrendered on October 19, 1781. Despite the fact that Congress had not yet forwarded the "Standard of the United States" for Washington's use, it is almost inconceivable that on such a momentous occasion, his greatest military triumph, some form of an American national flag would not have been in evidence.

But in this instance there is more than mere conjecture upon which to draw. Lieutenant Colonel John Graves Simcoe, who commanded the Queen's Rangers in the comparatively quiet British fortifications on Gloucester Point, was artistically inclined, and during lulls in hostilities he used his time to paint a watercolor of Yorktown during the siege (Pl. XII-32). The original of Simcoe's picture is now owned by Colonial Williamsburg, Inc., and it definitely shows a Stars and Stripes flag flying over the American works opposite his position. This banner has seven red and six blue stripes alternating, and in the blue union is "a pattern of figures, marks or, perhaps, stars in what seems to be a darker shade of blue. These are arranged in several rows (3 or 4) and definitely do not have the form of a circle."[13]

The flag pictured in Simcoe's painting may well have been the same to which St. George Tucker referred on October 9, 1781, in his journal of the Siege of Yorktown, when he mentioned that the "Continental Standard" was hoisted over an American battery.[14] Be this as it may, two officers of the Pennsylvania Line also noted that on October 19, the day of Cornwallis's surrender, an American detachment marched into Yorktown, took possession of the batteries, and unfurled "the American Flag."[15] A German mercenary with the British Army went further in recording this same incident: "The Americans hoisted a large flag here at Yorktown on the water battery, which had 13 stripes, which signified the 13 provinces of the United North American free states."[16]

Still additional evidence bearing on the use of a Stars and Stripes flag at Yorktown is presented in a "Plan of the investment of York and Gloucester" prepared by Major Sebastian Bauman, of the New York Second Artillery Regiment. An engraved copy of this plan in color, dated Philadelphia, 1782, is in the Phelps Stokes Collection at the New York Public Library (Pl. XIII-33).[17] At the bottom of it, below Bauman's delineation of the military lines, appears a rather elaborate cartouche with military equipment, accoutrements, and several flags, one of which, at the right side, has six white and five red stripes alternating. Two more stripes are probably obscured by the flag overdraped next left, which, if such be the case, would have made seven white and six red. The union is pale blue with faintly illustrated white stars arranged in no particular pattern. A letter from Bauman to Major General Alexander McDougall, dated October 24, 1782, presenting the latter with a copy of the plan, refers to "accuracy in the design" but goes into no further details.[18] Meticulous individual that he was, Bauman would probably never have given this particular flag the prominent place it occupies in his cartouche had he not been familiar with it, or if it was not actually used at Yorktown.

A Stars and Stripes flag with white stars arranged in a circle within a pale blue union, but otherwise identical with that shown in the Bauman plan cartouche, appears in the painting "Storming the Redoubt," by Eugene Lami, now exhibited in the State Capitol at Richmond, Virginia.[19] Lami did not execute this picture until 1840, but the similarity is interesting. Trumbull's painting of the Surrender of Yorktown shows a quite similar flag (but with eight red and eight white stripes, starting with a red stripe at the top), as does the group portrait of Washington, Lafayette, and Tench Tilghman at Yorktown, by Charles Willson Peale.[20]

Whatever the relative strength of these numerous claims which have here occupied our attention, there certainly seems to be sufficient evidence that varying forms of the Stars and Stripes were flown on land at different times and places during the Revolutionary War, whether as national or regimental standards, even though no such flags were officially delivered to Washington until 1783. Significantly, not a single one of those above described was the banner of seven red and six white stripes, with thirteen five-pointed white stars arranged circularly within the blue union, popularly conceived in story and legend as the handiwork of Betsy Ross.

CHAPTER 6 ★

The Second Stars and Stripes

THE CONTINENTAL CONGRESS, UNDER WHOSE AUthority the Revolutionary War was fought, constantly found itself beset by a sea of difficulties. Foremost among these was the task of maintaining an army and navy by which the independence hopefully proclaimed on July 4, 1776, might be achieved. Despite the efforts of Congress, Washington's troops often lacked many things essential to bare existence. Even the procurement of such equipment as drums and flags was delayed almost until the war's end.

Congress's Marine Committee understood, of course, the practical necessity for a flag to identify vessels at sea, and although positive records are lacking we may reasonably assume that it discussed the subject and that the Flag Resolution of June 14, 1777, creating the Stars and Stripes, was introduced with its knowledge and approval. Since no appropriation was required, nor any personal or political interest involved, the harried legislators resolved their problem without fuss or controversy.

So the Stars and Stripes was created. Like the nation, however, the newborn banner was an inchoate thing, fuller development of which came gradually with the passage of time. For such details as relative proportions of the flag, size of the union, design of the stars and their arrangement thereon, those who made our first flags were free, as has been shown, to exercise personal preferences. Less than two decades had elapsed, however, when a situation arose which the Congress in 1777 had not foreseen, and with which the individual flag maker was powerless to cope.

The United States of today was created by a slow fusing of separate and discordant political communities into one common whole. Com-

PLATE VII

22
These two flags appear in the Mondhare flag sheet published at Paris in 1781. The flag of the American Congress at the left carries a blue canton with 13 white stars (the hand colorist painted the top one as a French fleur-de-lis) and 7 red and 6 white stripes.

The drawing at the right shows the mercantile flag of the United States without canton or stars but with 7 red and 6 white stripes. *Courtesy John Carter Brown Library*

Flamme des
Etats unis
de l'Amerique
Autres Flamme
des Etats unis
de l'Amerique

23
The Mondhare flag sheet of 1781 shows these two United States naval pennants. *Courtesy John Carter Brown Library*

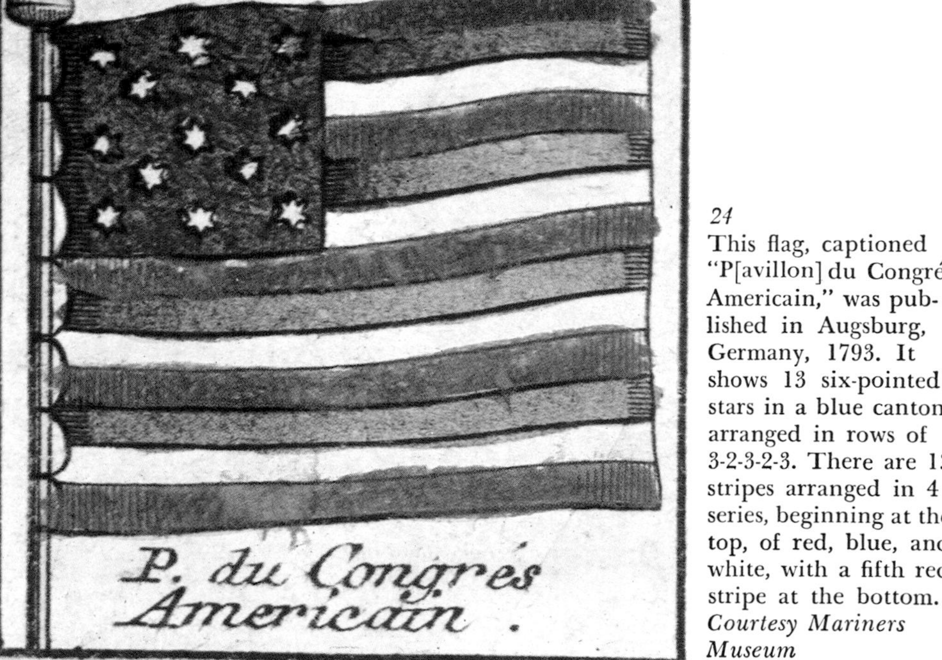

24
This flag, captioned "P[avillon] du Congrés Americain," was published in Augsburg, Germany, 1793. It shows 13 six-pointed stars in a blue canton, arranged in rows of 3-2-3-2-3. There are 13 stripes arranged in 4 series, beginning at the top, of red, blue, and white, with a fifth red stripe at the bottom. *Courtesy Mariners Museum*

25
This flag, captioned "P[avillon] Marchd des Etats unis de l'Amerique," has the same number of stripes arranged in the same order as the flag in No. 24, but has no canton or stars. It appeared in the same work as No. 24. *Courtesy Mariners Museum*

promising their special interests proved exceedingly difficult, and not until 1781, when the war was almost ended, were the Articles of Confederation finally agreed upon. Conflict between the large-State and small-State parties principally accounted for this long delay. Seven of the original States advanced claims, usually based upon their colonial charters, to land extending from sea to sea.[1] The six other States had no pretensions of this kind, and they naturally feared that when the western country came to be settled they would be overshadowed in wealth, population, and political power by their large-State neighbors. They also felt that since national independence was being achieved by common effort and sacrifice of all the States, the western lands should rightfully be owned by the national government, and administered by it for the general benefit of all.

The spokesmen of Maryland, in particular, were adamant champions of the small-State view, and they steadfastly refused to enter the Union until their demand for cession of the western country to the Confederation was met. At length, in 1780, New York, whose title to western lands was comparatively shadowy, offered to surrender her claim.[2] Thereupon, in October following, Congress adopted a resolution pledging that any lands thus ceded to the United States would be administered for the common benefit, and would be erected into new States, to be admitted to the Union as equal partners with those already existing.

With this important resolution the United States took the first positive steps in solving a problem which had baffled the genius of England's statesmen, whose fumbling precipitated the Revolutionary War. Where the British could think of no other answer to the colonial question than armed conquest and forcible submission, America now proposed to create self-governing States in her own western domain. As such, these States would tax and largely maintain themselves, and being equals in the Union would have a stake in remaining permanently loyal to it. This became the cornerstone of the American territorial system, and the basic political policy which made possible expansion of the Republic from thirteen original commonwealths to our present fifty.

Thus the Congressional resolution adopted in October, 1780, rendered obsolete the Flag Resolution of June 14, 1777, since the latter implied permanence of a Union having but thirteen States. Even before the war came to a close, plans were being eagerly discussed in the Continental Army and elsewhere for the settlement of a new State northwest of the Ohio River. This led finally to the Ordinance of 1787, enacted July 13, which created a single temporary government for the entire region bounded by the Great Lakes and the Ohio and Mississippi rivers, with provision for its division, as the progress of settlement warranted, into as many as five States.[3] The founding of Marietta followed quickly in 1788, and Ohio, the first State carved from the Northwest Territory, was admitted to the Union fifteen years later.

Long before this two other States had been added to the original thirteen, Vermont in 1791 and Kentucky in 1792. The first Stars and Stripes was now outgrown, and, like the Great Union Flag before it, had to be replaced by a more appropriate emblem. On December 23, 1793, Stephen R. Bradley of Vermont informed the Senate that "on Wednesday next" he would ask leave to introduce a bill "for altering the Flag of the United States." Wednesday next was Christmas Day, and there was no session of the Senate until the day following, when the bill was introduced and read. On Friday, the 27th, it was given a second reading, and on Monday, the 30th, was read for the third time and passed. The last day of 1793 saw the bill transmitted to the House of Representatives, where it was read twice and "committed" for further action.

Like the Flag Resolution of 1777, the newly proposed legislation was remarkably brief. In less than four lines of print it provided that beginning on May 1, 1795, the Flag of the United States should be "fifteen stripes, alternate red and white," with a union of "fifteen stars, white in a blue field" (Pl. XIV-34). Unlike the situation in 1777, however, there was now provision for recording the debates in Congress, as established by the new Federal Government instituted under the Constitution adopted in 1789. Legislative discussion on Bradley's bill, therefore, may still be read.

The debate upon this subject in the House disclosed high resentment toward the Senate for troubling it with the matter. Although the latter had passed the bill without discussion, the lower chamber, on January 7, 1794, resolved itself into a Committee of the Whole to deal with it, and fireworks began at once.

Goodhue of Massachusetts thought the bill "a trifling business, which ought not to engross the attention of the House, when it was its duty to discuss matters of infinitely greater importance. If we are to alter the flag from thirteen to fifteen stripes, and two additional stars, because Vermont and Kentucky have been added, we may go on adding and altering at this rate for one hundred years to come. It is very likely before fifteen years elapse we shall consist of twenty States. The flag ought to be permanent."

Lyman, also of Massachusetts, begged to differ with his colleague. He considered it of the greatest importance not to offend the new States. Thatcher, another Massachusetts man, shared Goodhue's sentiments, ridiculing the idea of being bothered with the bill, which he termed "a consummate piece of frivolity."

Opinion was ventured mildly by Greenup of Kentucky that it seemed important to inform the world that we now had two additional States. But he found himself squelched by Niles of Vermont, who curiously agreed with the Massachusetts detractors. Niles was sorry that the bill had even "for a moment" detained the House from worth-while matters of business. He did not think it worth the trouble of either adopting or rejecting, but as the shortest way out urged that it be promptly passed.

To this the committee agreed, and the measure then came before the House proper, where much the same lines of argument were again heard. Boudinot of New Jersey thought it important "to keep the citizens of Vermont and Kentucky in good humor" and feared that they "might be affronted" if the bill were defeated. Goodhue again deplored the proposed legislation as beneath the attention of the House, but since it must be passed, he begged as a favor that it might not appear upon the journal and go to the world as the first measure enacted by the present session. Madison and Giles, both of Virginia, hoped for passage, and Giles said he believed it very proper to preserve the idea of having the number of stripes correspond with the number of States, adding that expense of the change would be but trifling.

Smith of Vermont now joined his colleague Niles in a slashing condemnation of the bill. The change would cost him $500, and every vessel owner in the Union $60. He could not conceive why the Senate sent over such bills unless it was for lack of something better to do. He would indulge them, but wanted no more such alterations: "Let the Flag be permanent."

On the following day, after a third reading of the bill, an effort was made to amend it by adding the clause "to fix forever the Flag of the United States," and thus to preclude requests for future changes as new States were admitted. This proposal was voted down, and the bill was finally passed, on January 13, 1794, by a vote of 50 to 42.[4]

The debate upon this bill clearly indicates what the generation which created our national flag really thought about it. Obviously, there was no particular veneration for the Stars and Stripes, nor was the subject regarded as important. Such indifference is not hard to understand. In 1794 the United States was not yet a strong nation. Until 1789 it remained but a weak political confederation. As late as 1788, two of the original thirteen States (Rhode Island and North Carolina) had not yet joined the Union, and a third (New York) took no part in the first Presidential election. The Stars and Stripes had never been officially carried by the Army, nor would it be for another generation to come. There was no navy to display the flag abroad, and although it floated over some merchant ships and land fortifications, the vast majority of Americans never came in contact with it.

The sentiments expressed by members of Congress in 1794 undoubtedly reflected the feelings of their constituents with regard to the flag bill. When Senator Bradley forced the subject upon their attention they passed his proposed legislation as the quickest way of terminating a "trivial" discussion. Even so, the decision was close, and a change of four votes in the House would have meant rejection of the bill.

It can hardly be claimed that the framers of the Second Flag Act wrought either wisely or well. They showed but slight sense of dignity and no appreciation whatever of the Union so recently established on a new and firmer basis. Meanness of spirit and lack of vision characterized their debates, and the flag they adopted signally lacked that element of permanence for which some of them argued and voted. By 1794 it was clear that the creation of more new States was only a question of time. Were these to be forever denied representation upon the national banner? And if not, how could a flag of fifteen stars and fifteen stripes be considered permanent? Again, despite seventeen years of experience with the Flag Resolution of June 14, 1777, nothing was done to clarify exactly how the flag should be made.

Nevertheless, the banner of fifteen stars and fifteen stripes remained the United States national flag for almost a quarter of a century, during which the American Navy was reborn, three wars were waged with the Barbary States of North Africa, and American seamen repeatedly bested the enemy in an undeclared war with France. With these events the Stars and Stripes grew in prestige and historical associations.

26
This flag, really a pennant, appeared in the same work as Nos. 24 and 25. It is captioned "Autres Flamme des Etats unis de l'Amerique." This pennant has a blue canton with 13 six-pointed white stars arranged as in the flag shown in No. 24. To the right of the canton are 13 vertical stripes in sequence of red, blue, and white. To the right of them are three horizontal stripes, arranged from the top in a sequence of red, blue, white. The tapered end of the pennant splits at a point where the middle, blue, stripe ends and continues with two tails, red and white. *Courtesy Mariners Museum*

27
This flag is reputed to have been carried or present at the Battle of Bennington, just over the Vermont border, in New York State, on August 16, 1777. The original flag is preserved at the Bennington Battle Monument and Historical Society, Bennington, Vermont. It measures 10 feet long by 5½ feet wide. The top stripe is white rather than red. The blue field is 9 stripes deep, which is unique. The 11 stars are arranged in the form of an arch; two additional top corner stars make a total of 13 representing the full number of original States. Many authorities believe that this banner is the oldest known Stars and Stripes flag, that it is the first Stars and Stripes flag known to have been used by United States ground forces, and was the first Stars and Stripes flag raised in victory in the Revolutionary War.

Plate X

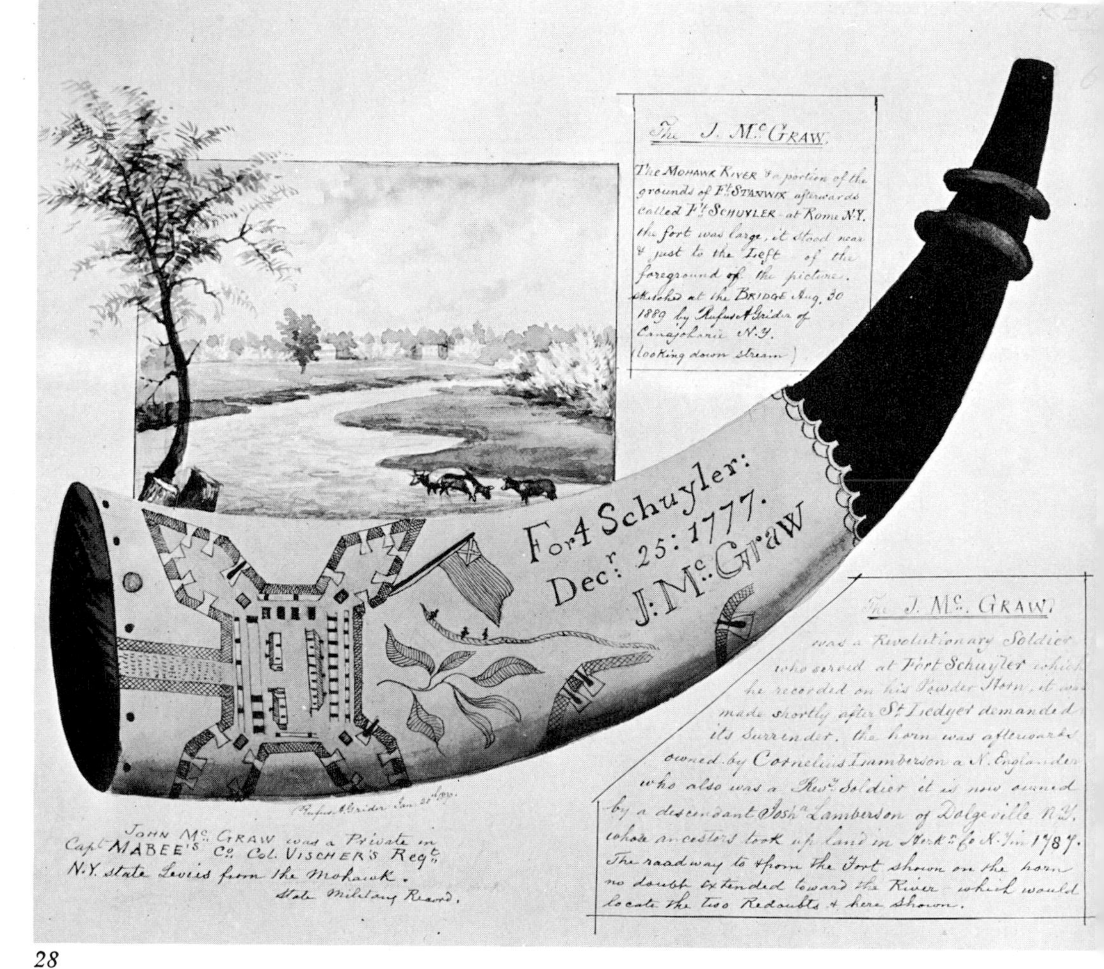

28

John McGraw powder horn carving showing flag at Fort Schuyler (formerly Fort Stanwix), New York. McGraw was a private serving in the New York Militia there in 1777, at the time of Col. Barry St. Leger's British and Indian campaign down the Mohawk Valley. This powder horn apparently was made in 1777. The flag engraved on it is McGraw's version of the Great Union design. *Courtesy New-York Historical Society, New York City*

CHAPTER 7 ★

The Star-Spangled Banner

For a dozen years ending in 1815, England and France were engaged in a duel to the death, devoting all their energies to winning the contest. In this conflict of giants the interests of neutral nations were ruthlessly disregarded, and since the United States was then the chief neutral in the world its commerce was preyed upon and its sovereign rights ignored. Belatedly, in 1812, the nation blundered into a three-year war with England, conducted by the Federal Government in a shamefully inefficient manner.

Yet some substantial successes were achieved. In particular, the tiny American Navy, from which so little had been anticipated that a plan was gravely proposed to use it solely for harbor defenses, put to sea and electrified the country by winning a surprising number of actions against the overwhelming might of British sea power. Under the flag of fifteen stars and fifteen stripes, Captain James Lawrence of the *Chesapeake* sailed to heroic fame and an untimely death in 1813, atoning for the disgrace of Captain James Barron in the same ship in 1807, who had been forcibly stopped and searched by a British warship, unable to make any defense because his guns were not ready. Under it the *Constitution* destroyed the *Guerrière* in August, 1812, and overwhelmed the *Java* four months later. When the War of 1812 came to a close, no more was heard of the impressment of American seamen, or the forcible seizure of American ships by the British Navy.

An important American achievement in this struggle was the creation of the song we know as "The Star-Spangled Banner." Today every citizen of the United States pays reverence to the national anthem, but this was not always true. The song, like the flag it celebrates, grew but slowly in public affection. Francis Scott Key, the author, never bothered to write down the story of how it came to be composed, or of how it was publicized and sung. Long after he had died, when his associates undertook to do so, their memories of the event were neither complete nor accurate. At length, in 1907, more than ninety years after "The Star-Spangled Banner" was written, a scholarly investigation of its history was undertaken, and the resulting report, published in 1909, sums up most of what is known of its origin and publication.[1]

As often in life, an affair insignificant in itself produced an undreamed-of result. In the summer of 1814 a British fleet and army entered Chesapeake Bay intent upon harrying the adjacent countryside. The admiral of the fleet was eager to capture or destroy the small American naval force which had thus far eluded his pursuit, while the general of the army intended to avenge upon his enemies certain outrages they were supposed to have committed along the Canadian border. With ridiculous ease General Ross thrust aside all opposition, and on August 24-25 captured and burned Washington.

Despite this complete victory, the British army suffered some loss in the Battle of Bladensburg, and its rapid movements compelled it to leave the wounded behind, where they fell into the hands of local citizenry. As always, also, there was some straggling by soldiers who may have been unable to keep up with the main force, or who turned aside from it in search of forage or plunder.

The village of Upper Marlboro is about seventeen miles distant from Washington. Someone carried to its people a false report of British defeat at Washington, whereupon a group of them promptly staged a celebration, "with copious libations," to mark the rumored American victory. The leader of this gathering was Dr. William Beanes, the local physician. While the merrymakers pursued their pleasant way, three British stragglers, "foot-sore, dusty, and weary," appeared upon the scene to beg a drink of water. Such at least is one family tradition, though another account represents that the stragglers were abusive and belligerent toward the Marlboro folk. Whatever the actual facts, the hilarious celebrators, urged on by Dr. Beanes, conveyed them to the village jail.

When news of this affair reached the British officers, they became angry, and before very long the lively Dr. Beanes found himself confined on board a vessel of war. The prospect of his deportation or other severe punishment alarmed his friends, and to avert such a fate they enlisted the aid of Key, an intimate acquaintance and successful Washington lawyer.

Accompanied by Colonel John S. Skinner, United States Government agent for arranging the transfer of prisoners, Key repaired to Admiral Cochrane's flagship, where both were courteously received. At first the admiral declined to admit that Dr. Beanes had any claim upon his forbearance, stating that his punishment ought actually to be more severe than what he had yet suffered. Colonel Skinner, however, produced a pouch of letters, written by British soldiers wounded at Bladensburg, extolling their excellent treatment received at American hands. This information tended to mollify Admiral Cochrane's attitude, and after some further discussion he finally agreed to release the prisoner.

Key and Skinner were entertained for several days aboard the British fleet, where, mingling freely with the officers, they learned of plans for an impending attack upon Baltimore. Because of this they were refused permission to return ashore until after the attack had been made, but were allowed to reboard the tender on which they had come out. It was from the deck of this boat that the two Americans witnessed the bombardment of Fort McHenry during the night of September 13-14, 1814. Late that night the cannonading ceased, and they remained in ignorance as to whether the fort had surrendered, or the British had abandoned their attack. "The dawn's early light" dissolved their fears, and as the day grew brighter it became apparent that the enemy fleet and army were engaged in preparations for departure.

There are two accounts of the writing of the song by Key, both recorded from memory by intelligent witnesses over a third of a century later. One of these was supplied by Chief Justice Roger Taney, a brother-in-law of Key, in 1856. The other account was written by Skinner himself.

Judge Taney related that some days after the bombardment Key came to him with a printed copy of "The Star-Spangled Banner," which he read and praised. Taney then asked Key

how he found time, in the scenes he had been passing through, to compose such a song? He said he commenced it on the deck of their vessel, in the fervor of the moment, when he saw the enemy hastily retreating to their ships, and looked at the Flag he had watched for so anxiously as the morning opened; that he had written some lines, or brief notes that would aid him in calling them to mind, upon the back of a letter which he happened to have in his pocket; and for some of the lines, as he proceeded, he was obliged to rely altogether on his memory; and that he finished it in the boat on his way to the shore, and wrote it out as it now stands at the hotel on the night he reached Baltimore, and immediately after he arrived. He said that on the next morning he took it to [Judge Joseph H] Nicholson to ask him what he thought of it, that he was so much pleased with it that he immediately sent it to a printer and directed copies to be struck off in hand-bill form.[2]

Skinner's firsthand narrative was recorded eight years earlier than Taney's relation, but both were the product of old-age memories. He remarks that having completed his business with the British he asked for leave to return home. Admiral Cochrane informed him that he must be detained until after the attack, but consented to his returning aboard the vessel on which he had come to the fleet. Skinner wrote:

It was from *her* deck in view of Fort McHenry, that we witnessed through an anxious day and night "The rocket's red glare, the bombs bursting in air;" and the song, which was written the night after we got back to Baltimore, in the hotel then kept at the corner of Hanover and Market streets, was but a versified and almost literal transcript of our expressed hopes and apprehensions through that ever memorable period of anxiety to all, but never of despair. Calling on its accomplished author the next morning, he [Key] handed it to the undersigned, who passed it to the Baltimore *Patriot,* and through it to immortality.[3]

In attempting to answer the question when, and under what circumstances, "The Star-Spangled Banner" was initially printed and first publicly sung, it is necessary to analyze a mass of conflicting testimony and tradition, none of which is contemporary, and most of which is untrue. The accounts of Judge Taney and Skinner, the two leading witnesses, are themselves contradictory in several important respects. Both agree that the poem met with instant appreciation, but Taney ascribes this to Judge Nicholson, while Skinner affirms that such praise was his own.

Whether the song was indeed "immediately" struck off by a printer it seems impossible to verify. We do know, however, that before many days passed it was printed as a broadside, and that on September 20 it appeared in the Baltimore *Patriot*. Next day the Baltimore *American* also published the poem, preceded by a 173-word introduction, all under the headline "Defence of Fort M'Henry." This introduction briefly recited the circumstances of Key's mission to the British fleet, his detention during the bombardment, and his composition of the song. The author's name was not disclosed, nor was any title given to the poem itself, merely the information "Tune: Anacreon in Heaven."

A week later, on September 27, 1814, the Washington *National Intelligencer* reprinted the Baltimore *American's* "Defence of Fort M'Henry" article, with this comment appended to the poem: "Whoever is the author of those lines they do equal honor to his principles and his talent." Thus Key's home-town editor had not yet learned that he was the author, while as late as October 19 the Baltimore *American* still withheld the secret. Apparently the song was first publicly sung and for the first time given its present title on that date, when the play *Count Benyowski* was performed in Baltimore. "After the play," it was announced in the press, "Mr. Harding will sing a much admired *New Song,* written by a gentleman of Maryland, in commemoration of the GALLANT DEFENCE OF FORT M'HENRY, called THE STAR SPANGLED BANNER." One authority suggests that Ferdinand Durang, a Baltimore actor, may have been the first person to sing the words of Key's poem in public, which if true would deny that honor to Harding. The family papers of Thomas Carr, a music publisher whose shop was at 36 Baltimore Street, in Baltimore, state that he was the first to release the words and music under the present-day title in 1814.[4]

The tune "Anacreon in Heaven" is not generally familiar to modern readers. Knowledge of it was widespread, however, in 1814, and the fact is clear that Key composed his poem in obvious imitation of the older song, from which he borrowed not only the melody itself, but also the meter and verse form.

Anacreon was a well-known lyric poet of Greece who, according to an ancient epigram, worshiped "the Muses, Wine, and Love." Toward the close of the eighteenth century a London social club was named, in his honor, the Anacreontic Society. This was a convivial and musical organization, admission to the ranks of which was eagerly sought by leaders of English society. The club song, "Anecreon in Heaven," written by John Stafford Smith, was rendered at every meeting. It became popular not only in England but also in Ireland, where, with different words, it served as a drinking song. Later it crossed the Atlantic. One of the earliest adaptations in America was the Boston patriotic song by Robert Treat (Thomas) Paine,* "Adams and Liberty," which appeared in 1798. Proof of the

* Not to be confused with the English-born author of *Common Sense.*

song's popularity in the United States is attested by the fact that it was here adapted to more than twenty different lyrics.[5] Thus Francis Scott Key utilized, as others before him had done, the familiar tune and meter, but instead of celebrating the delights of worldly dissipation he poured into his transformation one of the most remarkable patriotic outburts ever penned.

Whether Key's poem is good, considered merely as literature, must remain a matter of individual opinion. Historically, however, it expressed the revulsion and anger excited by the spectacle of armed invasion of the writer's homeland. Some of its lines are no longer valid history, and perhaps never were. With the restoration of cordial relations between Great Britain and America the third stanza became obsolete. More and more, as time passes, this is omitted when "The Star-Spangled Banner" is publicly sung.

Efforts made to supply additional or substitute verses from time to time have not been notably successful. One such stanza, written by Oliver Wendell Holmes during the Civil War, expressed current Northern sentiment toward Secession and preservation of the Union.[6] Another, published in 1931 by Colonel Harrison Kerrick, celebrates the dream of universal peace.[7] However appropriate its theme of "world friendship forever," in the present state of world tension it seems to be as much of an anachronism as Key's third stanza of 1814. All such efforts to add to Key's poem sentiments popular for the moment, but which the author himself could not even remotely have conceived, when he originally penned the song, are as futile as they are unwise. Of necessity, every poet must give expression to the feelings of his own time and place.

The original "Star-Spangled Banner" which Key saw still waving in the breeze over Fort McHenry early on the morning of September 14, 1814, is fortunately still preserved (Pl. XIV-35, Pl. XV-36). Circumstances surrounding the making of this historic flag, which originally measured thirty by forty-two feet, have never been fully determined. The Flag House Association, with headquarters in the old home of Mary Young Pickersgill, its maker, 844 East Pratt Street, Baltimore, holds a receipt for her labors on it. How long it took her to complete the work after a visit to her home by General John S. Stricker and Commodore Joshua Barney, who commissioned her to make the flag for Fort McHenry, is not known. However, it is evident from the receipt that she was paid $405.90 for her services on August 19, 1813. The material used was four hundred yards of first-quality handwoven wool bunting.

A letter written years later by Mrs. Pickersgill's daughter Caroline, addressed to Mrs. William Stuart Appleton, youngest daughter of Lieutenant Colonel George Armistead, who as a major commanded Fort McHenry in 1814, affords some explanation for the durability of this flag, even though penetrated by fragments from exploding bombs. In the letter, Caroline tells how her mother devoted particular attention to reinforcing the topping or heading of the flag, as might be expected from one of the best flag makers of that day.

For a number of years after 1814 the original "Star-Spangled Banner" remained in possession of the Armistead family. The flag bears upon it both Armistead's autograph and the date of the British bombardment. In 1861 his widow bequeathed it to Mrs. Appleton, and she in turn left it to her son, Eben Appleton, of Yonkers, New York, upon her death July 25, 1878. During this long period the family displayed their proud possession each year on September 13-14 to celebrate the anniversary of the historic attack on Baltimore. On one occasion, September 14, 1824, the battered old emblem was brought back to Fort McHenry in connection with a reception honoring General Lafayette.

Mr. Eben Appleton loaned the old flag to the Smithsonian Institution, at Washington, D.C., in 1907, where it was placed on official display for the first time. The loan was made an outright gift to the Smithsonian on December 19, 1912.

Finally, in 1914, much-needed preservative work on the flag was undertaken by Mrs. Amelia Fowler and several other expert needlewomen, who stitched the "Star-Spangled Banner" to a linen backing. It now measured twenty-eight by thirty-two feet. In doing this work of reinforcing they developed a new technique of using very small stitches, which were arranged in squares about a fourth of an inch each way in matching thread. Because of their tireless efforts, and the interest of others as well, the Fort McHenry Victory Flag, as it is sometimes called, was saved for posterity. It is now on permanent exhibit at the Smithsonian Institution.

CHAPTER 8 ★

The Third Stars and Stripes

WITH THE CLOSE OF THE WAR OF 1812, THE UNITED States entered upon a long period of peaceful domestic development. Forgotten were American failures in the conflict, while the memory of naval triumphs won by such seamen as Decatur, Hull, and Perry produced an exaggerated glow of national pride.

In such an atmosphere it was inevitable that the growing inadequacy of the flag should receive early attention. Even in 1794, when fifteen stripes and fifteen stars were specified for the official flag, one of the debaters in Congress had prophesied that within fifteen years the number of States would increase to twenty. Although this forecast was not realized, by 1816 there were eighteen States, and the early admission of still others was imminent.

The man chiefly responsible for the adoption of the third national flag was Peter H. Wendover, a representative in Congress from New York City. Beginning with the Congress which met in December, 1816, he persisted in his self-appointed task until the passage of a new Flag Act on April 4, 1818, crowned his efforts with success. The little we know of Wendover's career indicates that he was an individual of commonplace ability, whose sole claim to fame was his achievement in developing the flag which has now served the nation for over a century and a half. This is glory enough for one man, and as long as the Stars and Stripes continue to wave the name of Peter H. Wendover should be held in grateful remembrance.

On December 9, 1816, the same day that saw the admission of Indiana to Statehood, Wendover offered a resolution in the House calling for appointment of a committee to consider alteration of the flag. This resolution being carried by only a bare majority vote, he

PLATE XI

29
North Carolina Militia Flag, carried at the Battle of Guilford Courthouse, March 15, 1781. The original flag is preserved in the North Carolina Hall of History, Raleigh, North Carolina.

30
Flag of 3rd Maryland Regiment. This flag was carried by Lt. Col. John Eager Howard's 3rd Maryland Regiment at the Battle of Cowpens, South Carolina, January 17, 1781. It is made of a thin material similar to cheesecloth, measures a little more than 5 feet long and varies between 30 and 34 inches wide. This flag is preserved at the State Capitol in Annapolis, Maryland. *Courtesy State of Maryland*

PLATE XII

31
Stars and Stripes flag believed to have been flown at Fort Independence, Boston, Mass., in 1781, Revolutionary War.

32
This watercolor drawing by Lt. Col. John Graves Simcoe, commanding officer of the British Queen's Rangers at Gloucester Point, Virginia, in 1781, shows an American flag flying at Yorktown in 1781 during the siege operations. While the design of the flag is indistinct, it appears to have a blue canton with blue stars and 13 stripes, 7 red and 6 blue. The original watercolor is 5¼ by 21 inches in size. Although the stripes are well defined the blue canton is not. It carries a pattern of marks, figures, or possibly stars in what appears to be a darker shade of blue. They are arranged in several rows, three or four depending on the viewer's interpretation of what constitutes a row.. *Courtesy Colonial Williamsburg, Inc.*

refrained from pressing the subject at once, but three days later explained his reason for proposing the inquiry, particularly dwelling on the fact that although the legislation of 1777 and 1794 provided for one star and one stripe for each State, there were now five States unrepresented on the flag.

Other reasons for dissatisfaction with the existing flag were developed in subsequent months. In 1816-18, as forty years earlier, the national ensign was still primarily a naval banner, and among fundamental considerations involved was its visibility at sea. This was brought up very early in the debates by Representative Taylor of New York, who stated that naval men had informed him that the Stars and Stripes could be recognized at sea farther than the flag of any other country. The addition of more stars and stripes would render it less distinct to distant observation, and this he wished to prevent. Taylor therefore favored restoring the thirteen stripes and thirteen stars, and making that design of the flag permanent.

The subject was finally referred to a select committee with Wendover as chairman, and on January 2, 1817, this committee rendered its report, recommending that the number of stripes be reduced to the original thirteen, but that the stars be increased to the number of existing States with provision for future addition of one more star upon admission of each new State. This was the short session of Congress, and amid the pressure of other business that body adjourned on March 5 without acting further in the matter.

Soon after the new Congressional session opened, however, on December 16, 1817, Wendover renewed his resolution of the year before for appointment of a committee of inquiry upon the expediency of altering the flag. This time, in support of the measure, he commented on the fact that individual Stars and Stripes in general use agreed neither with the law nor with each other. In proof of this he called attention to the flags flying at the Navy Yard and over the buildings in which Congress sat, one containing nine stripes and the other eighteen, "and neither conforming to the law." For once objectors were silent, and Wendover's motion was adopted without opposition. Early in January, 1818, his committee submitted its report and bill to the House, which on March 24 following considered it at length in Committee of the Whole.

Here again Wendover led the argument for changing the flag. After relating the now familiar story of the significance of the thirteen stars and thirteen stripes as representing the original States existing in 1777, he pointed out that within thirteen months after the alteration of 1794 the admission of Tennessee to Statehood once more made the flag incongruous and out-of-date. Since it was obviously impracticable to change the general design of the flag whenever a new State came into the Union, or to go on adding indefinitely to the number of stripes, and as there was no need of twice advertising the number of States, the committee proposed to revert to the thirteen stripes as representing the number of original States, and to have the stars in the blue union correspond with the whole number of existing States. The difficulty of occasionally adding a new star to the flag would be slight, obviating at once needless expense for new flags and having the flag grow to unwieldy proportions. As evidence of present lack of uniformity, the speaker reminded his listeners of the differences between the fifteen-stripe flag required by law and several flags then flying over Washington.

On two other points, Wendover's comment was also instructive. The committee had deemed it desirable to include in its bill a requirement that the stripes be horizontal. This was the case, as a matter of custom, in the existing flag, but a banner with perpendicular stripes would be no less conformable to law. On the other hand, the committee wished to leave the arrangement of stars in the union to the discretion of individual flag makers, "whether in the form of one great luminary, or, in the words of the original Resolution of 1777 'representing a new constellation.' "

Several amendments to the committee's bill were proposed. One of these favored leaving the thirteen stripes to represent the original States but having the stars show only the additional States later admitted to the Union. Another provided for fixing the number of both stars and stripes at thirteen each. These attempts to change Wendover's proposal being rejected, his measure was then adopted without further serious opposition.[1] This legislation remains today the legal charter of the flag, and its importance justifies setting forth all its provisions, which were as follows:

AN ACT TO ESTABLISH THE FLAG OF THE UNITED STATES

SECT. 1. *Be it enacted, &c.,* That from and after the fourth day of July next, the flag of the United States be thirteen horizontal stripes, alternate red and white; that the union have twenty stars, white in a blue field.

SECT. 2. *And be it further enacted,* That on the admission of every new State into the Union, one star be added to the union of the flag; and that such addition shall take effect on the fourth of July next succeeding such admission.[2]

So the third act prescribing the Flag of the United States, still in effect today, was adopted on April 4, 1818 (Pl. XVI-37). Comparing it with the legislative determinations of 1777 and 1794, one notes that the only significant innovations were to fix the number of stars to correspond with the number of existing States, to provide for the number of stripes remaining permanently at thirteen, horizontally arranged in legalization of established custom, and to arrange for addition of stars to the union as new States were admitted to company with the old. Arriving at these simple changes had required forty-one years of time.

The Congress of 1818, however, like its predecessors in 1777 and 1794, was content merely to describe the flag in broad outline, still leaving to individual ingenuity or fancy the determination of many details about design and dimensions. Thus no specific statement was made concerning the number of points on the stars or their arrangement on the union, and although Chairman Wendover had stated that one of the main objectives of his act was elimination of the many variant flags then in use, this result was not accomplished. As a matter of fact, the committee deliberately refrained from prescribing how the stars should be arranged. Indeed, practically another hundred years rolled by before the President of the United States, by executive order, produced that uniformity in the design of the Stars and Stripes whose absence had been so pointedly deplored.

No one can justly deprive Peter H. Wendover of the honor due him for steering the 1818 Flag Act through Congress. There was another individual, however, whose contribution on the point of design should be noted. Samuel G. Reid was a native of Connecticut who became a sailor at the age of eleven and master of a ship at twenty. In September, 1814, he embarked from New York as captain of a privateer, the *General Armstrong*. Caught by three British warships in the Portuguese harbor of Fayal, he made a valorous defense against hopeless odds, finally scuttling and abandoning his vessel, which the victors then burned. America rang with Reid's praise and he became a popular naval hero. Many years later, in 1859, when pressing upon Congress a claim for losses sustained in destruction of the *General Armstrong,* he advanced the further allegation that he "did make and design the present Flag of the United States," and for this service modestly requested a vote of thanks.

Taking up Captain Reid's claim about the flag design, a joint resolution of Congress stating that satisfactory evidence of his achievement had been presented was referred to the House Committee on Naval Affairs, which rendered a report on the subject, concluding that correspondence between him and Wendover indicated

> that if the suggestion was not originally that of Captain Reid, although such was probably the case, yet he was intimately connected with the movement and much contributed to settle the matter; and that he procured to be made in his own family, without compensation, the first flag which was displayed, after the passage of the act, from the dome of the Capitol.[3]

Various letters between Wendover and Reid, submitted to the committee in support of the latter's statement, have since been published.[4] The first is dated February 13, 1817, and the last April 13 of the following year. They indicate a rather close and cordial cooperation between the two men in the flag change enterprise right from the beginning of this period. A postscript to Wendover's letter of March 24, 1818, has the following interesting passage:

> I this day had our flag measured up and down the staff. It is fourteen feet and four inches, but it ought to be eighteen feet hoist, and floating in the air in proportion say twenty-seven feet; all this you know better than I do. Now, Jack, I ask as a favor that you will be pleased to inform me, as soon as convenient, what a flag of that size will cost in New York, made for the purpose, with *thirteen stripes,* and *twenty stars forming one great luminary, as per pasteboard plan you handed me*. And if the bill passes the Senate soon, it is probable I shall request the captain of the late General Armstrong to have a flag made for Congress Hall under his direction. Please inquire as to the cost of materials, &c., and write me soon, that Congress for their firm support of the bill may, before they adjourn, see the banner raised.

The sequel to this inquiry was that Mrs. Reid made the new flag as requested, and at two o'clock in the afternoon of April 13, 1818, it was hoisted over the Capitol dome. The twenty stars in the union were arranged in "one great luminary" forming a huge composite star.[5] All this would not actually be legal, under the act so recently passed, until "from and after the fourth day of July next," but in view of the attendant circumstances Wendover's eagerness to display the new national emblem in public may be excused. Later that same year, President Monroe was to stipulate that the stars should be arranged in four equal, parallel rows of five each.[6]

PLATE XIII

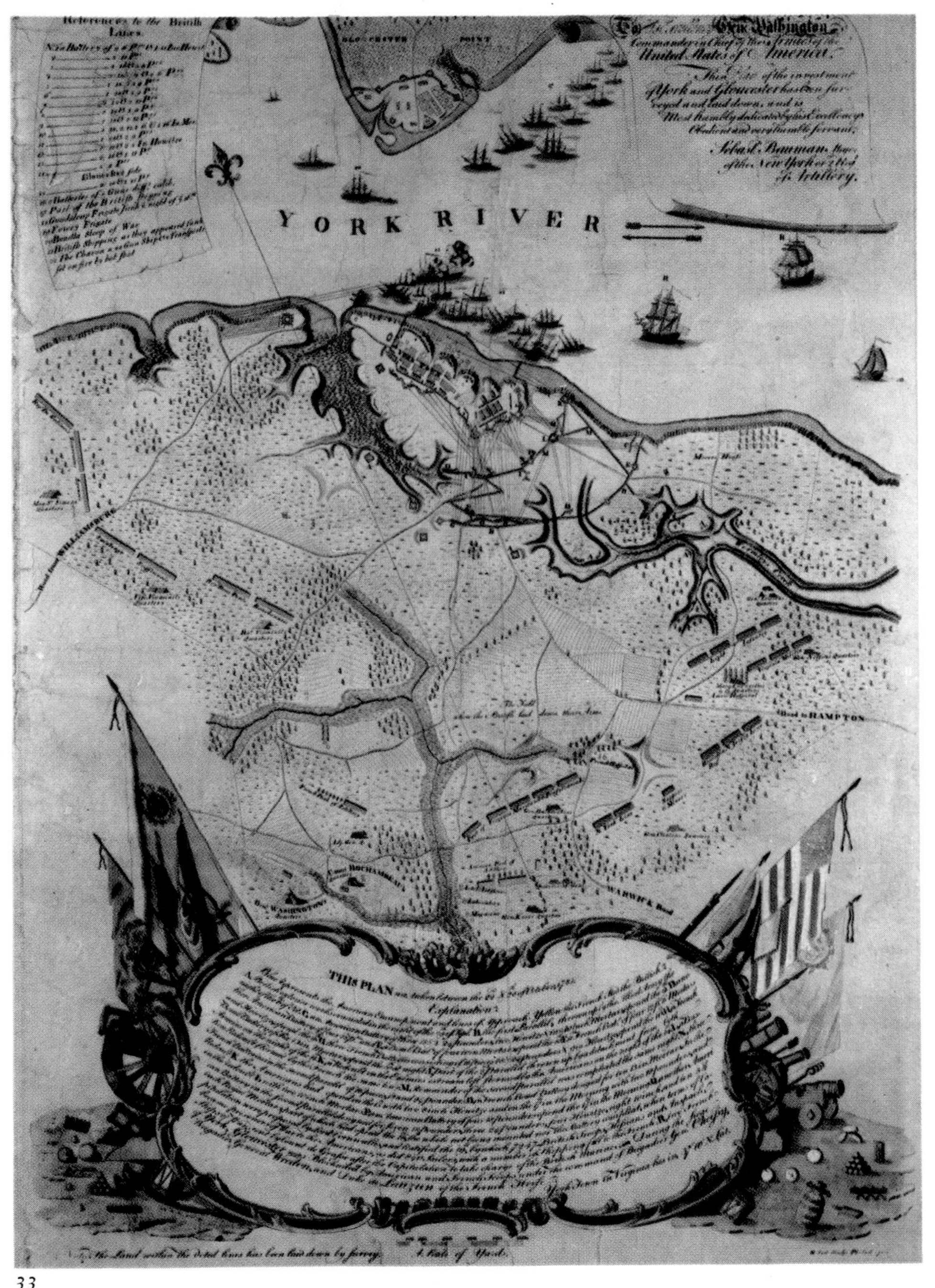

33

Map drawn by Maj. Sebastian Bauman of the investment of York and Gloucester harbors (Yorktown, Virginia), October, 1781, showing United States flag in cartouche at bottom right. *From New York Public Library, Phelps Stokes Collection. Courtesy American Heritage Book of the Revolution*

PLATE XIV

34

Second Flag of the United States, 1795-1818. This was the first United States Flag to be carried across the continent to the Pacific. Meriwether Lewis and William Clark carried it on their expedition of 1804-1806. It was also the flag flown over Fort McHenry at Baltimore on September 13-14, 1814, that inspired Francis Scott Key to write "The Star-Spangled Banner."

35

Although precedent was thus established for future Presidential actions concerning design details of the flag, a subject on which the basic act of 1818 was largely silent, a confused lack of uniformity still prevailed for many years thereafter. Preble quotes the following contemporary statement to illustrate this:

> On the 4th of July, 1857, a gentleman amused himself by noting the various designs displayed on vessels, hotels, and public buildings in New York. The majority of the ships had the stars arranged in five horizontal rows of six stars each, making thirty stars in all,—thirty-one being the proper number at that date. Most of the foreign vessels, including the Cunard steamers, had them arranged, as heraldists would say, semé, that is, strewn over the union. Some had one large star formed of thirty-one small stars, and this style prevailed at places of public amusement and over the hotels of New York and Jersey City. Other vessels had them in a lozenge, a diamond, or a circle. One vessel had one large star composed of smaller ones, within a border of the latter; another carried the thirty-one stars in the form of an anchor; and yet another had this anchor embellished with a circle of small stars.[7]

Observations similar to the above could probably have been made in many other parts of the United States, more or less through the whole nineteenth century. The Flag Act of 1818, therefore, while representing a considerable forward step in development of the Stars and Stripes, was but one in a long series of events which shaped and influenced its growth. Not for years to come would the flag be generally uniform in design and proportions all over the nation.

PLATE XIV *35*

The Star-Spangled Banner was the Garrison Flag of Fort McHenry, Baltimore, Maryland, during the British bombardment of the fort on September 13-14, 1814. It is a flag of 15 stripes and 15 stars, the standard design from 1795 to 1818. After the successful defense of Fort McHenry, the flag was presented to Lt. Col. George Armistead, who had commanded the Fort. It passed to his daughter, Georgianna. In 1912, her son, Eben Appleton, sent it to the United States National Museum, Smithsonian Institution. Originally, the flag measured 30 by 42 feet, but when repaired in 1914 its surviving part measured 28 by 32 feet. The flag was made in Baltimore by Mrs. Mary Pickersgill at her home (preserved and now known as the Flag House), assisted by her daughter, Mrs. Caroline Purdy. They received $405.90 for their work. The flag has been displayed folded in a cramped display case and few people have seen the entire flag. A special display area in the Smithsonian's new Museum of History and Technology will show the flag full length. *Photograph by B. Anthony Stewart, Courtesy National Geographic Society*

CHAPTER 9 ★

Early United States Army Flags

STRANGE AS IT MAY SEEM, THROUGHOUT AMERICA'S early history as a nation the Stars and Stripes was not used officially in the United States Army. Although called the Flag of the United States, it had been adopted for use at sea, and both in the debates of 1793-94 and those of 1817-18 in Congress over proposed alteration its suitability as a naval banner was the consideration chiefly stressed. Since many more years were still to pass before the Stars and Stripes was introduced into the Army, this was perhaps natural enough. Yet so contrary to present-day thinking is this conception that it is difficult to understand.

The Treaty of Paris concluded in 1783 awarded to the United States all the region lying between the Ohio River and the Great Lakes, westward to the Mississippi. By another of its provisions, the British agreed to remove their armed forces from within the area conceded to the new nation "with all convenient speed." Along the seaboard this was done, and it was the expectation of Congress and General Washington that the forts along the Great Lakes—Oswego, Niagara, Detroit, and others—would also be yielded to American control.

But difficulties soon arose over the treaty. The northwestern Indians, most of whom had sided with Great Britain in the Revolutionary War, and who had not been consulted in making terms of peace, refused to give up their country to the United States and demanded recognition of the Ohio River as the boundary between the Americans and themselves.

A state of war therefore continued on the western frontier. Obviously the settlers must be protected, and the hostile tribes subdued, if peace was ever to be established on a firm footing. Yet the Confederation Congress, with strange disregard of ordinary common sense, proceeded as rapidly as possible to disband the Continental Army, as a result of whose efforts national independence had been won. By the spring of 1784 this army had dwindled to a single infantry regiment and some few companies of artillery, seven hundred men in all. Even this puny force was viewed by the politicians as a menace to the "liberties of a free people," and on June 2 of that same year it was dismissed, except for eighty men retained to serve as caretakers of military stores at West Point and Pittsburgh.

A non-existent army had no need for flags of any kind. In a short time, however, Congress was compelled to appeal to the several States for levies of militia, to be enlisted for twelve months, so as to garrison the northwestern posts which the British were expected to evacuate. Meanwhile, the Indians continued their attacks upon the western frontier, and a few months' experience taught anew the lesson that untrained militia forces were quite unsuited for prolonged and arduous military service. In 1785, therefore, Congress began to create a new regular army, although it still avoided the name. Under the leadership of Secretary of War Henry Knox and General Josiah Harmar, plans were made to enlist seven hundred three-year soldiers for frontier service. Two companies of artillery were added to the lone infantry regiment in 1786. Notwithstanding these efforts, effective strength of the national forces was still only 595 men when the new government under the Constitution took over in 1789.[1]

Although the new federal establishment created at that time was woefully weak, it could not avoid the duty of defending its citizens, and since the northwestern Indians repeatedly declined overtures of peace, President Washington reluctantly prepared to subdue them by force. In the autumn of 1790 General Harmar led an army of 300 regular soldiers and 1,100 militia levies northward from Cincinnati against the Indian towns at the headwaters of the Maumee River. Although the regulars fought bravely, the militia ran away, and the campaign proved a humiliating failure.

A second regular regiment was now raised, and in 1791 Governor Arthur St. Clair led another invasion of the Indian country. His defeat on November 4 at what is now Fort Recovery, Ohio, was among the most crushing in American military annals. It also led to the appointment of a third commander, Anthony Wayne, to conduct the war, and incidentally to a thoroughgoing reorganization of the American Army.

During these years of feebleness and defeat the Army somehow obtained a flag, the design of which, though modified, is still in use. The career of General Knox assumes particular significance in this connection. One of the most trusted and capable officers in the Revolutionary struggle, he became Secretary of War under the Confederation Congress in 1785, and at President Washington's request continued in this capacity with enlarged powers under the new national government established in 1789. Like St. Clair and Wayne, therefore, who had also served as Revolutionary War commanders, Knox was a connecting link between the Continental Army of that period and the new military organization. He undoubtedly knew about Washington's discussions with the Board of War in 1779 concerning the design of a standard for the Army, and was probably familiar, also, with the actual standards so belatedly delivered to the Commander in Chief in 1783. When the problem of fixing upon a standard for the new United States Army presented itself, it would thus have been natural for Knox to draw upon his own past personal knowledge and experience, recalling the standard adopted for the Continental Army a few years earlier.

So much for conjecture. Turning to the actual record, in Washington's letter of September 14, 1779, there is agreement upon a standard having "the Union and Emblem in the middle," with the additional proviso that the regimental number and the name of the State to which it belonged ought to be inserted "within the curve of the serpent" (see Chapter 2). Although the Army regulations contain no description of regimental flags prior to 1834, the first flag carried by the lone infantry regiment from about 1787 to 1791 is still preserved (Pl. XVII-38), as is the flag provided for the new regiment created in 1791.[2] Both flags have the "Union and Emblem" in the center conformable with the design agreed upon by Washington and the Board of War in 1779, though neither shows the "curve of the serpent."

The design of these earliest United States Army banners is of decided importance to this story, since from them were evolved the flags still borne by American infantry regiments, and until recent years by the cavalry as well. The legislation of 1791 authorized the raising, in addition to the 2nd Infantry Regiment, of two regiments of six-month levies, to be known as the First and Second Levies. The

Army therefore had four regiments and four regimental flags when St. Clair's defeat on November 4, 1791, stimulated Congress to more decisive action.

From the resulting new legislation emerged the Legion, a more streamlined regular army with an authorized strength of 5,120 men. The four former regiments were now transformed into four Sub Legions, into which the Legion as a whole was divided. Under General Wayne's stern leadership the Legion became a highly disciplined military force, able to cope with any enemy of comparable size.

Flags naturally had to be provided for the Legion, and on September 13, 1792, Wayne wrote from Pittsburgh to Secretary Knox that "Standards, Batt^{n} and camp colors are much wanted for parade and maneuvering."[3] This appeal brought the reply, eight days later, that "four excellent large standards" had been forwarded to Cincinnati in 1791 for the four regiments which existed at that time; they were made of silk, and "expensive," and with some changes of lettering and coloring should answer perfectly as Sub Legionary standards. Battalion and camp colors would be prepared as requested. Finally, if the President should approve, a "Legionary Standard" having a bald eagle formed of silver and large as life would be provided, or, if this idea were not adopted, "something [else] of the flagg kind" would be devised.

But Wayne, like his Commander in Chief in the Revolutionary War, was doomed to wait weary months for his standards. On March 30, 1793, he reminded Knox of his promise to send them forward, to which the latter replied on April 6 following that there were "four elegant standards" at Fort Washington (Cincinnati) which had never been used, and which should answer the purpose of Sub Legionary flags. On the related subjects of battalion and camp colors, as with respect to the Legionary Standard with its silver eagle large as life, Knox remained conveniently silent.

Thus the regiments of 1791 never saw their elegant colors, which still remained at Fort Washington. On July 25, 1793, still without the wished-for flags, Wayne directed his Quartermaster General to remove their former regimental markings and in place thereof to substitute the words "1st Sub Legion," "2nd Sub Legion," "3d Sub Legion," and "4th Sub Legion." Apparently this was done, for on August 16 following General Wilkinson at Fort Hamilton wrote to Wayne that he had entrusted Captain Lewis with the standards of the late First and Second Regiments "with orders to perish the whole detachment, or deliver them in safety to your Excellency's hands."[4] The flags were duly received by Wayne, and Captain Lewis lived out his term of service. One of these four Sub Legionary banners is still preserved at West Point. The three others have long since disappeared from public view and probably no longer exist.[5]

As a result of Wayne's conquest of the northwestern Indians, the British Ministry at last decided to evacuate the line of western posts within the borders of the United States. The transfer was to be made on June 30, 1796, but the arrival of this date found the British forces more ready to yield the posts than the Americans were to receive them. Fort Miamis (near Toledo) and Detroit were occupied by United States troops on July 11, and the remaining forts were taken over during that summer and the early autumn following.

American rule and American flags thus arrived together on the Great Lakes, but it is uncertain that the latter included the Stars and Stripes. As we have already seen, the national emblem is supposed to have been flown over Fort Independence, at Boston, in 1781 (see Chapter 5). A sketch of Fort Washington, made in 1791 by Major Jonathan Heart, also prominently features a Stars and Stripes flag, and if accurate this indicates its early garrison use in the Northwest Territory.[6] Similar use at the Lakes posts, therefore, is a not altogether unreasonable conjecture.

Of particular interest in this connection is a letter written by Dr. Charles Brown, who came to Detroit with an advance detachment of American troops on July 11, 1796. In that letter, dated September 28 following, Dr. Brown informed a friend that the departing British had left all in good order, "and the very staff that elevated their union now displays the strip[e]s of America." Was he here talking about the Stars and Stripes? One can only guess, for his meager description fits equally well "The American Stripes," that banner of thirteen alternate red and white stripes, its folds sometimes adorned with an undulant rattlesnake, which was especially popular with American naval and merchant vessels in Revolutionary War days, and which continued to be flown on both land and sea for many years thereafter (see Chapter 1).

Still another interesting item which bears on the question at issue is contained in a printed volume in the Army War College Library listing expenditures of the Quartermaster's Department. This is an entry from Detroit in 1798 showing the purchase from James Abbott and Son, local merchants, of some "red, blue, and white ratinett [a thin woolen fabric], linen, thread, etc., for the garrison," the cost being $39.99. It might be fairly assumed that these materials were to be used in making a garrison flag; and that since the cloth was "red, blue, and white," the Stars and Stripes were intended. Again, however, as in so many like situations, it is difficult to be sure of what actually came to pass, the evidence not being entirely conclusive in any direction.

With the arrival of General Wayne in mid-August, 1796, ancient French-British Detroit became for a time the headquarters of the United States Army, which its commander now undertook to reorganize. The Legion was abolished, and in its stead reappeared four regiments of infantry, supplemented by two companies of dragoons and a corps of artillerists and engineers. Restoration of the regiment as the basic Army unit was also marked by a return to Washington's plan for regimental flags in the Revolutionary War, that is, to equip each regiment with two flags, one the national color and the other a distinctive regimental flag. How this design was defeated until after the close of the conflict with Great Britain, has already been observed. The four regiments sent against the northwestern Indians were provided with national colors only, on which the regimental designation had been inscribed; and these same flags, with such inscriptions suitably altered, had been used as the Sub Legionary banners of Wayne's Legion. From 1796 onward the infantry regiments were supplied with both national colors and regimental standards.

In 1802 the Army passed through another reorganization, and in the years following to 1812 still other changes were made in the national military establishment. Flags of the infantry regiments followed a rather uniform pattern, however, until 1834, the national color being blue, with an eagle and the shield of the United States at its center; above, the stars of varying number and design; and below, a scroll bearing the regimental name and number. The oldest such numbered national color still in existence is that of the 1st Regiment of Infantry, now preserved at West Point (Pl. XVII-39). Regimental colors, by contrast, were of plain white or yellow silk, with the regimental designation on a scroll in the center.[7] The colors of the artillery regiments exhibited the same general design as the infantry flags, while the calvary, which for some curious reason was long discriminated against, had only the blue standard, whose design was but little altered until 1895.

In Chelsea Royal Hospital, London, one may see today the battle flags of the 4th U.S. Infantry, captured by the British at the surrender of Detroit, in August, 1812. That unit's national color, now much dilapidated, was originally a blue silk flag, bearing the eagle and stars as described above, with fifteen stripes on the shield. Although some of the stars are now missing, it seems highly probable that their original number was also fifteen (PL. XVII-40).

It is interesting to observe that while the Stars and Stripes continued to represent but fifteen States until the passage of the 1818 Flag Act, the regimental national colors often accorded recognition to States more recently admitted to the Union as early as the War of 1812. Thus the flag of the 1st Regiment of Light Artillery had both seventeen stars and on its shield seventeen stripes (PL. XVIII-41). The same number of stars and stripes were shown on the national color of the 14th U.S. Infantry,[8] and this seems to have been the general rule for the Army national colors of this period.

CHAPTER 10 ★

The Stars Join the Army

THE YEAR 1834 MARKED SEVERAL OUTSTANDING DEvelopments in the history of the American Flag. It witnessed the first significant change in the colors carried by the United States Army since the reorganization of 1796; saw the first official attempt to prescribe the details of the flag; and for the first time the Stars and Stripes was admitted to the Army.

Issued from time to time, the General Regulations for the Army govern existence and operations of that organization. In 1834, for the first time, these condescended to notice and describe the Army flags then in use. The garrison flag was to be the Stars and Stripes, made of bunting, with thirteen horizontal stripes of red and white. The blue union, in the upper quarter near the staff, was to extend one-third the length or fly of the flag, and downward to the lower edge of the fourth red stripe, counting from the top; and in the union a star was prescribed for each existing State.

Fifty-seven years after the birth of the Stars and Stripes, therefore, a few important specifications governing its design were officially ordered. This regulation applied only to the Army, however, and neglected to mention such significant matters as the relative dimensions of the flag, or the size and number of points on the stars, and their arrangement in the union.

Also for the first time, in 1834, an official statement was supplied concerning the number and design of the infantry flags, though no radical change was made from the practice long in force. The national color of the infantry regiments continued to be a blue flag with the arms of the United States in silk at the center and the regimental name and number on a scroll beneath the eagle. The second, or regimental flag, was to be white, with the name and number of the regiment in gold or yellow silk on a blue scroll in the center. These two flags were to be six feet on the staff and six and one-half feet in fly, surrounded by fringe of yellow silk and equipped with cords and tassels of black and yellow intertwined. Unlike the infantry and artillery, cavalry regiments were to have but a single standard, two feet, three inches on the lance and two feet, five inches in fly, with a yellow fringe. The field was to be blue, with the arms of the United States at the center, and the regimental number and name on a scroll beneath the eagle. Except for its smaller dimensions, the cavalry standard was thus pretty much a replica of the infantry national color.[1]

The major innovation of 1834 was in the artillery flags. In this case, as with the infantry, each regiment was to have two silk colors, six feet on the pike and six and one-half feet in fly. The regimental standard prescribed was a yellow flag with yellow fringe, having two crossed cannon at the center, with the letters "U.S." above and the regimental number and name beneath; and cords and tassels of red and yellow silk intertwined. The national color, by contrast, was to be the Stars and Stripes, the same as the garrison flag, with the regimental designation inscribed in gold letters on the center stripe. With this change, the national emblem had at long last gained official entrance to one branch of the Army.

The regulations of 1834 also prescribed camp flags for the infantry and artillery regiments, and company guidons for the cavalry. The former were to be eighteen inches square on an eight-foot pike, white for the infantry and red for the artillery, and with the regimental numbers inscribed on them. Cavalry guidons were to be swallow-tailed, the upper half red, the lower half white, dividing at the fork. The letters "U.S." were inscribed in white on the red upper half and the company number in red on the lower white portion. Dimensions of the guidons were two feet, three inches on the lance and three feet, five inches from the lance to the end of the swallowtail.

Several of these regulations of 1834 remained in force for more than fifty years, and some of them for a much longer period. Until 1886 yellow continued the artillery regimental color; the cavalry regiments were equipped with the single blue standard until 1895; and the red and white cavalry guidons remained in use for over a century after they were first introduced.

To enact laws or issue regulations is one thing; to observe their provisions, particularly when the subject involved is the American

Flag, can be quite another. So it may have been with the Army in the years following promulgation of the 1834 regulations. There being no existing white regimental color from this period, the possibility confronts us that none was issued; nor is it known, either, that the artillery and cavalry colors prescribed in 1834 were actually issued, or if issued what was their precise design. Why the Stars and Stripes was made the national color for the artillery, while the infantry and cavalry continued under their old flags of blue, likewise remains a mystery.

Some light is shed upon these questions, however, by a few Army banners believed to date from the later 1830's. The 2nd Dragoon Regiment was organized in 1836, and its standard, which may be as old as this, is a flag of deep blue, apparently complying with the 1834 regulations for cavalry standards. In 1861, when this regiment became the 2nd U.S. Cavalry, it received a new flag similar in design to the earlier one described above. Now preserved at West Point (Pl. XVIII-42), that banner is in the opinion of Admiral Gherardi Davis, competent historian of the American Flag, the "handsomest pattern" ever adopted by the United States Army.[2]

Another interesting flag, supposed to have been preserved but which cannot now be located,[3] was that of the 4th U.S. Infantry, probably belonging to the years 1834-36, since it apparently had twenty-five six-pointed stars, and Michigan, the twenty-sixth State, was admitted to the Union in January, 1837. Indications are that this was the national color of the regiment until 1841, after which it became the regimental flag, so continuing in use, if the record is correct, throughout the first half of the Civil War. It exhibited the same general design as the blue infantry colors succeeding those in use prior to 1834, but unlike those earlier banners the eagle held in its beak a red ribbon on which was the motto "E Pluribus Unum"; the red scroll below the eagle was more elaborate; the shield had but thirteen stripes; and the letters "U.S.," formerly inscribed on its chief, were no longer in evidence.

The General Regulations for the Army issued in 1841 introduced a most significant change in the infantry colors. The old regimental standard of yellow or white, used respectively since 1796 and 1834, was now discarded. First applied to the artillery in 1834, the Stars and Stripes now became also the national color for infantry regiments; their long-established blue national color, bearing on its field the arms of the United States, was henceforth made the regimental standard. This arrangement remained unchanged for more than a century. Design of the latter flag, moreover, has been widely approximated for the flags of the various States, nearly one-half of which show the State arms centered on a blue field, usually fringed with yellow.

No further regulations were issued by the War Department with respect to Army flags until 1847, and no important changes came about until 1862. Meanwhile the Mexican War of 1846-48 was fought, and the regular regiments, chiefly involved in that conflict, carried colors of 1841 or earlier issue. Again the possibility of non-compliance with the existing regulations is presented, for at West Point are preserved several old-type yellow regimental banners supposed to have been used in the Mexican War. Unless this identification is erroneous, yellow colors were obviously retained for many years, contrary to the 1841 regulations.

No further change in the Army's colors was made until 1862. Many regiments continued to carry the colors issued prior to 1861 throughout the Civil War, while others exchanged them for new flags designed in accordance with the General Regulations issued in 1862. The artillery regimental colors adopted in 1834 retained the same general design until 1886. Illustrative is the 5th Artillery's regimental flag of 1861, having two gold cannon crossed on a yellow field, red ribbon and scrolls, with letters, edging, and other ornamentation in gold.[4]

The most notable innovation of 1862 was the replacement of the red-and-white cavalry guidon of 1834 with a new one, the design of which approximated the Stars and Stripes.[5] This marks the first use by the cavalry of a banner even approaching the national color, and herein lies yet another refutation of widespread popular belief that the Stars and Stripes was officially carried in battle by the Army from 1777 onward.

In still another respect, compliance with the legal provisions establishing the national flag was exceedingly slow. The Flag Resolution of 1777 and the Flag Acts of 1794 and 1818 all prescribe white stars. Yet for a long period the stars were commonly silver, and for some years during and following the Civil War gold stars were employed. Although none of the successive flag legislation prescribed arrangement of the stars in the union or specified the number of points they should have, custom early settled upon placing them in horizontal rows, and eventually upon stars having five points each. For more than half a century after the birth of the Stars and Stripes, the Army's regimental flags exhibited six-pointed stars about as often as five, while during the Civil War an oval arrangement of the stars in the union became the temporary vogue.

An unusual change in United States Army flags was introduced in 1866, when for the first time both battalion and national colors were prescribed for the engineers.[6] In this instance the national color was to be the same as that for the infantry, with the exception that gold letters were used for the battalion name. The battalion color was to be a scarlet flag of conventional dimensions (six feet on the staff, and six and one-half feet in fly), with a castle depicted in the center, underneath which in silver letters were inscribed "U.S." and "Engineers." A fringe of white, and cords and tassels of red and white intermixed, completed the specifications. To the unknown creator of this beautiful flag, so striking in appearance and original in design, we owe a debt of gratitude. A flag believed to be the first battalion color of the engineers ever issued is preserved at Governor's Island, New York.[7]

The first change in the color of a regimental flag since 1841 was made in 1886, when the artillery flags were changed from yellow to scarlet.[8] In 1887, apparently associated with this change, the cavalry —which for at least three-quarters of a century had borne the small blue standard similar in design to the infantry colors—was now, for the first time, given both national and regimental flags.[9] The national color became the Stars and Stripes; while the regimental color was of yellow silk, with the arms of the United States at the center, and underneath this the regimental name and number in yellow letters on a red scroll. Another red scroll, held in the eagle's beak, bore in yellow letters the motto "E Pluribus Unum," over which were thirteen white stars, surmounted by an arc of diverging sun rays, also in white. A fringe of yellow silk surmounted the fly. Both the national and regimental colors were to be three feet on the lance and four feet in fly.

Thus the United States Cavalry gained the Stars and Stripes as its national standard 110 years after the birth of the flag. More correctly, it would have done so had the order of April 13, 1887, been complied with. For some reason, unknown or unacknowledged, such was apparently not the case until a new order on the subject was issued in 1895.[10]

Also in 1895, the size of all flags except those of the cavalry was reduced. For almost 100 years these standards had measured six feet on the staff by six and one-half feet in fly. They were now cut down to four feet, four inches on the staff and five feet, six inches in fly. Even with this reduction the United States Army colors remain larger than those of military forces in most European nations.

Changes in the colors made since 1895 will be noted only briefly. The regulations of 1901 altered the inscription on the artillery colors, leaving the design unchanged. These are also the last regulations under which appeared the eagle with outstretched wings, featured on infantry and cavalry colors for nearly a century. Sweeping changes were inaugurated, however, by the regulations of 1904, in the regimental colors of the entire Army.[11] The regimental designation was removed from the field of its national color and placed instead on a silver band on the staff or pike. On all regimental or battalion colors the United States coat of arms, with a scroll beneath bearing the regimental name and number, was prescribed. For the engineers, the battalion color remained scarlet, as before; for the artillery corps, also, the color was scarlet; for the infantry, blue; and for the cavalry, yellow. The insignia of the engineers in white silk and the crossed cannon of the artillery in yellow were placed beneath the national coat of arms on their respective corps and battalion colors.

The United States Marine Corps is as old as the Navy itself, two companies of Marines having accompanied the expedition of Commodore Hopkins on his cruise to the West Indies in the spring of 1776. What the early flag of the Marines was, or indeed whether they had any, is unknown. Their oldest existing flag is said to have been painted by Joseph Bush, of Boston, in 1840-43.[12] The field of this standard has in chief a blue shield, and in the upper part an eagle in flight, sustaining a golden anchor with ropes, while in the background are thirteen five-pointed stars arranged in a circle.

Another early Marine flag, dating from the Mexican War, is supposed to be the second-oldest in existence. Its field is blue, like the cavalry and infantry regimental colors of the period; the union has an eagle with outspread wings, beneath which is the United States shield, from whose chief extends a scroll bearing the motto "E Pluribus Unum"; and around the whole, in circular arrangement, are twenty-nine five-pointed stars.[13] In 1876, nineteen years in advance of the cavalry and thirty-five years later than the infantry, the Marines were given the Stars and Stripes as their national color, the standard hitherto carried by them becoming now the Marine Corps flag.

On June 12, 1956, President Eisenhower issued an executive order creating an official flag for the United States Army, the design of which had been recommended to him by the War Department. This new standard is four feet, four inches in hoist by five feet, six inches in fly, made of white silk or rayon, and having a yellow fringe two and one-half inches wide. In the center of the flag is the central design of the seal of the Department of the Army (without the Roman numerals) in ultramarine blue, above a scarlet scroll with the designation "United States Army" in white, and with the Arabic numerals "1775" beneath the scroll. The order further provides for streamers representing each officially recognized campaign in which the Army has participated, each streamer to be embroidered with the name and year of the campaign. Thus, after a lapse of 180 years, the Army had at last obtained a distinctive standard.

CHAPTER 11 ★

Some Stories and Legends

THE FALLIBILITY OF HUMAN MEMORY IS WELL KNOWN. With the passage of time and frequent retelling of some past incident, recitals of events tend to depart more and more from their original form. Moreover, when descendants of the original narrator or other third parties undertake to relate them, incomplete knowledge of what they suppose, or recall, that they were told intensifies the process, until finally a tale that is largely or even wholly fanciful replaces the true story.

Other factors also assist in developing historical myths and errors. All trained historians are familiar with these and endeavor to base their own work upon original records pertaining to the subject they have in hand. Many persons do not have access to primary sources of information, or even when the latter are available have no leisure time for studying them. So historical stories and legends develop, gain popular acceptance by reason of their usually colorful or sentimental character, and with passing years tend to displace the truth altogether.

Strongest and most persistent of all legends about the flag is the one associated with Betsy Ross. Born Elizabeth Griscom, this now famous lady was a Philadelphian who married John Ross near the beginning of the Revolutionary War. He was accidentally killed in January, 1776, and she subsequently remarried a second and a third time.

From these marriages Betsy had seven daughters, whose descendants were numerous. Among the latter was William J. Canby, a grandson of Mrs. Ross, who was born in 1825. Canby appeared before the Pennsylvania Historical Society in 1870 and read a paper

36
This painting by Percy Moran shows the artist's conception of "The Star-Spangled Banner" flying over Fort McHenry as viewed by Francis Scott Key from a position in Baltimore Harbor. This painting now hangs at the Star-Spangled-Banner House Association Headquarters at Albemarle and Pratt streets, Baltimore, Maryland. *Courtesy Peale Museum, Baltimore, Maryland*

Plate XVI

37
Third United States Flag, 1818, the first flag under the Act of Congress, passed April 4, 1818, providing for the addition of one star for each State admitted to the Union.

which for the first time unveiled to the world a family tradition.[1] Briefly summarized, his story related that in June, 1776, Robert Morris and George Ross (the latter a signer of the Declaration of Independence and an uncle of Betsy's deceased first husband), constituting a committee appointed by Congress for the purpose, visited Mrs. Ross in her Philadelphia shop, accompanied by General Washington, and upon being admitted to her rear parlor disclosed that they had come to engage her to make a flag. Being a seamstress, Canby continued, his grandmother had often been visited by Washington before, had made shirt ruffles and performed other tasks for him, and the Commander in Chief was therefore familiar with her skill.[2] Although Betsy had never made a flag, she told her distinguished guests that she "would try," and apparently from this point onward she assumed rather efficient control of the occasion. The visitors had a rough drawing of the flag they wanted—the Stars and Stripes—and under the direction of Mrs. Ross, Washington sat down and redrew it. She explained that there should be a symmetrical arrangement of the stars, and that these should be made with five points, not six. The objection that this would prove difficult was quickly overcome when Betsy, using her scissors and a piece of folded paper, demonstrated the ease with which a five-pointed star could be cut out. After she had proposed some other changes, also accepted by the committee, the visitors departed. In due season the wished-for flag was made (Pl. XX-44) and then exhibited to Congress by Washington with this explanation, quoted later in another connection (see Chapter 12 for a discussion of the significance of the flag's colors): "We take the stars from heaven and the red from our Mother Country, separating it by white stripes, thus showing that we have separated from her; and the white stripes shall go down to posterity representing liberty."

Critical examination of the facts reveals that although Washington was actually in Philadelphia from May 22 to June 5, 1776, conferring with Congress on matters affecting general prosecution of the conflict with Great Britain, the Declaration of Independence had not yet then been adopted, and until that step was taken there could certainly be no very logical reason for replacing the Great or Grand Union Flag with a national banner of new design. Committees of Congress were appointed and we have the record of their names, their functions, and their membership; but no committee on the flag existed at that time, and no record of the claimed action or any report of such a body has been found. Despite this lack of evidence that it ever really happened, the Betsy Ross story has found its way into American folklore and remains even today the most widely held misconception about the flag.

While there is no substantiation for the legend that Betsy Ross was responsible for the first Stars and Stripes, one point about her deserves mention. It is a fact, recorded in the Pennsylvania Archives, that she was paid for making colors for the Pennsylvania Navy in May, 1777.[3] It is entirely possible that this fact led later generations of her family to claim that she made the first Stars and Stripes.

Some of the most ingenious fictions about the flag were manufactured by Augustus C. Buell, an industrious biographer of John Paul Jones, as recently as the year 1900. For a time even the world of scholarship was deceived by his audacious fantasies, and since their exposure gullible or uninformed writers have continued to incorporate them in their narratives.[4]

One of these deceptions foisted upon Jones is this vainglorious statement: "That flag and I are twins, born in the same hour from the same womb of destiny. We cannot be parted in life or in death. So long as we can float, we shall float together. If we must sink, we shall go down as one!"[5]

To provide suitable setting for this boastful declaration, its inventor has altered the plain historical record by printing together the Flag Resolution of June 14, 1777, and the resolution which followed it appointing Jones as commander of the *Ranger,* asserting that these two distinct enactments were "joined in one resolution." Furthermore, if Buell's fabricated statement ascribed to Jones means anything at all, it must signify that he was appointed to the Navy "in the same hour" the Flag Resolution was passed. This does not tally with the facts. Jones had been an American naval officer since December, 1775, and on June 14, 1777, he was merely assigned to the command of another ship.

More romantic, however, is another fabrication of the same biographer concerning the imaginary history of the first Stars and Stripes. This relates that when Jones went to Portsmouth to assume command of the *Ranger,* a bevy of girls held a quilting party and "from slices of their best silk gowns," and with their own "dainty hands," made such a flag and presented it to him to be hoisted on that vessel on July 4, 1777. If we may believe the sequel, this same banner was later transferred to the *Bon Homme Richard,* which Jones took as his flagship in 1779.

Since we know that Jones did not assume his new command until July 12, 1777, the alleged July 4 ceremony surely anticipated the actual event. Even more enterprising was Buell's exploit in inventing the five young women who, as members of the quilting party, sewed the imaginary flag. One of them, Helen Seavey, a bride of but a month, went so far as to sacrifice her wedding gown to supply material for the thirteen white stars. The author of this concoction further explained that when Jones returned to America in 1781 he informed one of the maidens that it had been his most ardent desire to bring the flag home and return it to the "fair hands" of its makers; but that when the *Bon Homme Richard* was about to sink, two days after her victory over the British frigate *Serapis* on September 23, 1779, he "could not deny to the dead on her decks, who had given their lives to keep it flying, the glory of taking it with them."[6]

Hollywood at its cleverest could scarcely improve upon a story like this, yet it has been accepted as truth by some historians of the flag. One such writer "presumes" that the banner "made from material so beautiful, yet so fragile and ill-suited to battle with Atlantic storms, was reserved for the Captain's cabin, while one of more robust texture took its place."[7] In Portsmouth, as elsewhere, Buell's fiction was readily credited, and a society called the "Portsmouth Quilting Party" was organized to commemorate the original band of maidens. It terminated somewhat abruptly when a careful investigator later disclosed that the five thoughtful and industrious girls were mere figments of the author's imagination.[8]

Although not the mythical flag of Buell's relation, the Stars and Stripes did fly from the masthead of the *Bon Homme Richard,* and Jones's own account of his fight with the *Serapis,* already referred to in Chapter 4 above, indicates that it was indeed lost, having been carried away by a cannon shot.[9] Eighty-three years after the event, however, when all the participants were dead and gone, the story was sprung upon the world that this historic banner, far from being destroyed, had actually been saved by one James B. Stafford, a midshipman on Jones's flagship, and that it was presented to him by the "Marine Committee" of Congress in 1784, along with other trophies, in recognition of his "meritorious services thro the late war."[10]

After Stafford's death, as the story goes, the flag with this purported history passed to his widow and daughter, and was exhibited at various Civil War Sanitary Fairs and at the Philadelphia Centennial of 1876, a piece of it having meanwhile been scissored off for presentation to President Lincoln. Eventually, through the agency of President McKinley, it was given to the Smithsonian Institution in Washington, D.C., where it is still preserved and was for many years displayed as the *Bon Homme Richard* flag. Now much mutilated, the Stafford banner is at present six feet, five inches in fly and five feet, seven inches on the staff, with stripes varying in width from four to five and one-quarter inches, and the union is twenty-eight by thirty-five inches in size.[11] A published illustration shows twelve five-pointed stars arranged in four rows of three each.[12]

Stafford was a reputable Revolutionary War seaman and himself never advanced the claim here discussed, while the family narrative supporting it bristles with contradictions and known misstatements of fact. The roster of all the officers and crew of Jones's ship does not contain the name of Midshipman Stafford. This omission is explained in the family story by saying that he went to sea on the *Kitty,* an American privateer, in 1776; that the *Kitty* was taken prize by a British man-of-war; and that Jones captured the latter a few days before his fight with the *Serapis;* whereupon Stafford, twice a prisoner within ten days, served in the battle between the *Serapis* and the *Bon Homme Richard* on September 23, rescued the Stars and Stripes flag of the *Richard,* and in so doing was cut down by the sword of a British officer. The truth is that Jones's own report, made to Franklin on October 2, 1779, clearly establishes that before meeting the *Serapis* he neither fought nor captured any British man-of-war. Stafford himself, when applying for a pension, stated only that he had served on the privateer *Kitty* from 1776 to 1781, and as a midshipman on the American ship *Alliance* from 1781 to 1783. During this latter period of service the *Alliance* fought engagements with several British armed vessels.

While it is apparently true that Stafford's shoulder blade was actually severed by a saber stroke, and that he did in fact obtain a Stars and Stripes flag, somehow or other, before his death in 1838, he left no written record of how or when either was acquired. There is only his family's word, therefore, on these interesting points. How questionable this is may be judged from the circumstance that his wife was born in 1775 and did not become Mrs. Stafford until September 27, 1793, fourteen years after the events described. Certainly her knowledge of any Revolutionary War battles in which her husband might have participated was not very immediate, and at best could have been based only on his or others' recollections a long time later. Finally, if the family story were true, why did not Stafford himself mention having served on the *Bon Homme Richard* in 1779, when he applied for a pension after the war, and why also did the roster of that illustrious vessel not contain his name?

The principal "evidence" which has led many people to credit this tale is a supposedly authentic letter addressed to Stafford from Philadelphia on December 13, 1784, informing him that the "Marine Committee" had decided to bestow upon him, in recognition of his "meritorious services" as already noted, " 'Paul Jones' Starry Flag, of the Bon Homme Rich[d] which was transferred to the Alliance'—A boarding sword of said Ship & a Musquet captured from the Serapis." The author concluded with advising Stafford that if he would "write to Captain John Brown at the yard, what Ship you wish them sent to N. Y.—they will be forwarded to you." A printed facsimile of the letter, reduced by half, shows the writer's signature as James Meyler, but a certified copy in the collections of the Pennsylvania Historical Society, made from the supposed original, gives the signer's first name as John.[13]

This is the letter which at one time satisfied officials of the Smithsonian Institution that the so-called Stafford banner was actually flown on the *Bon Homme Richard* in 1779. How authentic is that document? It appears somewhat curious, in first instance, that "Paul Jones' Starry Flag" should not have been reserved for presentation to the great American naval hero himself, rather than offered to a minor subordinate whom he neither listed as a member of his crew nor mentioned in his report of the *Richard's* battle with the *Serapis.* Is it not strange, also, that the letter makes no mention of Stafford's having gallantly saved the flag, but refers only to his "meritorious services thro the late war"? Or again, why has no other contemporary written record ever been found relating to this alleged transaction? These and similar pertinent questions are not easily answered. That the James or John Meyler letter to Stafford was in all likelihood spurious seems evident from subsequent action taken by the Smithsonian Institution. In response to an inquiry from Milo M. Quaife in 1942 the Associate Director of that organization stated that its Curator of History had become convinced, about fifteen years earlier, that the Stafford flag was not properly authenticated, since which time it had been kept in storage.[14]

Another romantic story about the national banner was told by Elizabeth Montgomery in 1851. This represents that her father, captain of the brig *Nancy,* which sailed for the West Indies under English colors in March, 1776, upon making port there, and learning about the Declaration of Independence, promptly had a Stars and Stripes flag made and hoisted it to the masthead of his vessel. Returning home, the account goes on, he found himself hotly pursued by a British fleet, whereupon he abandoned ship and blew up the brig. Unfortunately for its claimed validity, the Montgomery narrative has one fatal chronological defect: the *Nancy* was in fact destroyed, but the date of her demise was June 29, 1776, at which time the Declaration of Independence had not yet been adopted.[15]

CHAPTER 12 ★

More Fictions and Myths

CONSIDERATION HAS ALREADY BEEN GIVEN IN CHAPters, 2, 3, and 4, and particularly Chapter 5, to some of the most widely circulated claims, myths, and legends concerning the Stars and Stripes, especially to the allegation, almost universally believed, that it was officially carried as a national banner in land battles of the Revolutionary War. As has been shown, the Stars and Stripes was at no time supplied to the Continental Army by Congress before the close of that conflict, nor was it apparently intended for such service. Instead, it was created for use at sea as a naval standard, and not until almost every Revolutionary War soldier had passed away was it first officially admitted to one branch of the United States Army as a battle flag (see Chapter 10, where official designation of the Stars and Stripes as the national color of the artillery, in 1834, is discussed). This does not rule out, of course, certain probable and even proved unofficial uses of variant forms of the flag in land engagements before that time, as discussed in Chapter 5.

Another widespread misconception concerns the significance of colors used in the Stars and Stripes. Popular orators, flag "historians," and sentimental writers have played fast and loose with this theme, the statements of some often squarely contradicting those advanced by the rest. Obviously not all of these conflicting claims can be true, and actually none of them are. One writer affirms that the blue stands for heaven, "as it did in the Scottish flag of 937 A.D.," while the white represents the Navy, and the red the Army.[1] Not to be outdone, another author of "a manual of patriotism for boys and girls" affirms that the colors of the flag "trace their ancestry back to Mount Sinai, when the Lord gave Moses the Ten Commandments and the book of the law, and they were deposited in the Ark of the Covenant within the Tabernacle whose curtains were of scarlet (red), white, blue, and purple." He further explains that the red in the Stars and Stripes stands for courage, the white for liberty, and the blue for loyalty.[2]

Still another interpreter reports that the red stands for the nation's wars, the white for the years of peace, and the blue for faith in God.[3] Until quite recently the official *Handbook* of an important American youth organization instructed its thousands of readers: "The Blue of my Flag represents Justice like the eternal blue of the star-filled heavens—its White is for purity, cleanness of purpose—of word or deed—its Red is the red life blood of brave men and women, ready to die or to worthily live for our country." Fortunately the most recent issue of the *Handbook*[4] omits this and considerable more misinformation about the Stars and Stripes contained in earlier editions, and even evaluates the Betsy Ross flag-making story as only "according to tradition." On the other hand, it continues to perpetuate the notion that the stars were arranged in circular fashion on the union of the flag down to 1795, to credit the mistaken idea of its general use in Revolutionary War battles, and to repeat other errors as well. Almost thirteen million copies of this particular *Handbook* were printed from 1910 to 1952, providing perhaps the most potent source of factual misconceptions about the Stars and Stripes. Statements like those quoted are not history, but sentimental inventions. They should be recognized as such.

Many writers seek to find in the flag's colors some heraldic significance, bolstering their argument with analogy drawn from the adoption by Congress, on June 28, 1782, of the Great Seal of the United States. These are two entirely different things, neither really comparable with the other. The seal is admittedly a heraldic device, and as affirmed by the report which its designers submitted to Congress, white signifies purity and innocence; red, hardiness and valor; and blue, vigilance, perseverance, and justice. But the Flag Resolution was passed five years earlier by another group of men, and that action was far removed from the business of heraldic art.

Considering the veneration in which the memory of George Washington is held, it is not surprising that more or less ingenious efforts should be made to associate the Father of His Country with the flag. In this connection a spurious quotation has been invented which represents him as saying: "We take the stars from heaven, and the red from our Mother Country, separating it by white stripes, thus showing that we have separated from her; and the white stripes shall go down to posterity representing liberty." A *Flag Book* issued by the United States Marine Corps states that these words were uttered on the fanciful occasion "when the Star Spangled Banner was first flown at the head of the Continental Army." Others identify it with the unfurling of the Great Union Flag at Cambridge, Massachusetts, on January 1, 1776, blithely ignoring the fact that there were no stars in the union until enactment of the Flag Resolution of June 14, 1777. Again, this quotation is identified with the imaginary report made by Washington to Congress upon the result of the alleged "Flag Committee's" conference with Mrs. Betsy Ross. All these associations are incorrect. In response to an inquiry on the subject, the chief bibliographer of the Library of Congress, where the bulk of Washington's papers are housed, had the following to say: "We have had occasion before to search for this statement [as quoted above]. . . . We have been unable to find that Washington ever said or wrote it."[5]

Yet another fiction has been spun which ascribes the design of the flag to the Washington family coat of arms. The latter is a heraldic device consisting of the following elements: (1) the crest, a raven of natural color issuing out of a golden ducal coronet, and (2) a silver shield crossed by two red bars, above which are three spur rowels, also in red.[6] To be sure, the spur rowels look exactly like five-pointed stars, and the heraldic word "argent," for silver, was also sometimes interpreted to mean white. That is as far as any comparison with the Stars and Stripes really goes. There is absolutely no documentation for anything more.

Inventors of history are never content, however, with truth alone, but must further adorn and embellish it. In this particular case, the myth maker was an English poet and philosophical dabbler, Martin F. Tupper, who was eager to promote the cause of Anglo-American good will.[7] In anticipation of the United States Centennial Year, 1876, he composed a drama, *Washington,* wherein it was represented that Benjamin Franklin while in England had discovered the Washington coat of arms, which he later induced Congress to incorporate in the design of the new national flag. Thus this coat of arms, "magnified and multiplied," became "our glorious national banner." Although poet Tupper's motives were good, his pretended history was pure imagination. Franklin, at his diplomatic post in Paris, had nothing to do with the passage of the Flag Resolution on June 14, 1777, nor was the Continental Congress concerned with perpetuating the art of heraldry.

Recent widespread publicity was accorded this myth by Winthrop W. Aldrich, American Ambassador to Great Britian, in September, 1955. In a speech accepting the home of Washington's forebears on behalf of the United States, he described the family coat of arms as consisting of "a shield with three stars and two stripes surmounted by an eagle with lifted wings," and then continued: "Who can resist the conjecture that here at Washington Old Hall is the true origin of the Stars and Stripes and the great seal of the United States government?"[8] Thus easily did the raven in Washington's crest become a quite different bird, and sentimental assumption again leave its mark. The ambassador's comments in this and other respects may have been highly pleasing to his Anglo-American audience, but they were then, and still are today, wholly without historical basis.

Another misconception concerns the arrangement of the stars in early fabrications of the Stars and Stripes. This is popularly conceived to have been thirteen five-pointed white stars fixed in a circle on the blue union (Pl. XX-44). As we have seen, however, in Chapter 4, American naval flags differed from that design, and the ensigns flown by John Paul Jones's two ships, the *Alliance* and the *Serapis,* had their thirteen stars arranged in parallel horizontal rows, the former in 3-2-3-2-3 order, the latter in order of 4-5-4. Again, as explained in Chapter 5, no Stars and Stripes standards were officially furnished to the Continental Army by Congress before the close of the Revolutionary War; while those which may conceivably have been used in land engagements show wide variation in both the arrangement of the stars and their number of points. Trumbull's paintings of the Battle of Princeton (January 3, 1777) and the Surrender of Burgoyne at Saratoga (October 17, 1777) both show twelve stars in the form of a square and a thirteenth in the center; and Peale's painting of Washington at the Battle of Trenton has a blue flag with thirteen six-pointed white stars in a circle, with no red or white stripes (Pl. XIX-43). The Bennington Flag (August 16, 1777) had eleven stars in an arch around the numeral "76," with two more stars in the upper left and right corners of the union; the Third Maryland Regiment banner said to have been carried at the Battle of Cowpens (January 17, 1781) displayed twelve stars in a circle and the thirteenth in the center; the Guilford Courthouse Flag (March 15, 1781) had thirteen blue stars arranged in parallel horizontal rows on a white union in 4-3-4 order, with two more stars to the right of these, midpoint between the rows; and the Stars and Stripes apparently flown at Yorktown (October, 1781) featured the stars either irregularly arranged, in three or four rows, or twelve in the form of a square and the thirteenth in the center. (See text and notes on Chapters 4 and 5.) These obvious differences indicate all too clearly how far removed Revolutionary War practice actually was from the concept of thirteen five-pointed white stars in a circle, even as respects those few instances in which the record offers any documentation whatever for use of the Stars and Stripes in that conflict. In this connection it must again be observed, however, that since the Flag Resolution of 1777 was silent on the subject, one arrangement of the thirteen stars on the union was as valid as any other.

The general public notion about the stars having been fixed in a circle on the early Stars and Stripes seems to have sprung mainly from wide circulation of two popular paintings made in the last quarter of the nineteenth century. About the year 1875 an Ohio carriage painter produced a humorous Fourth of July offering which he entitled "Yankee Doodle." Redrawn and renamed "The Spirit of '76," it swept the country, becoming familiar to almost every American who lived in the decades immediately before and after 1900. The flag, prominently displayed in this picture, has the stars arranged in a circle. This conception of the original design became further fixed in the minds of millions of Americans following distribution, just at the close of the nineteenth century, of hundreds of thousands of copies of another painting, Charles H. Weisburger's "Birth of Our National Flag," which showed Betsy Ross in the act of displaying the mythical first Stars and Stripes made by her to George Washington and his companions. On the flag in Weisburger's picture, quite possibly in imitation of "The Spirit of '76," the stars are also arranged in a circle. Suffice it to say here that historical truth was dealt a crushing blow by these two paintings, the erroneous notion to which they gave birth having been perpetuated in uncounted illustrations appearing in school textbooks and other respectable publications. What actual evidence survives today all argues against a circular arrangement of the thirteen stars on the union.

A statement frequently made, though wholly inaccurate, affirms that the Stars and Stripes is the oldest national flag in the world. This assertion is evidently based upon the assumption that it is permissible for the flag of the United States to retain its identity while undergoing quite considerable changes through the years, although such retention is denied the flags of other countries. As described in Chapter 1, the Union Flag of Great Britain evolved from the cross of St. George, adopted in the later Middle Ages. Only by regarding its birthday as 1801, when the cross of St. Patrick was added, can the British Union be said to be younger than the Stars and Stripes. Applying this same reasoning to the American Flag, it would actually be one of the most recent national flags on earth, if not at this writing indeed the youngest, since a forty-ninth star for Alaska was added on July 4, 1959, and the fiftieth star for Hawaii took its place on the union on July 4, 1960.[9]

Another popular idea concerning the flag is the statement that each State is represented by a particular star on the union. Children in school are mistakenly urged to learn to recognize the star of their own State. In support of this fancy the further fiction is invented that the thirteen original States became States in the Union at the time and in the order of their ratification of the Constitution.[10]

The first thirteen States were born, however, on July 4, 1776, when they declared their independence of Great Britain. They existed for a dozen years before the Constitution was adopted, and instead of being "admitted" to the Union they created it. Moreover, until President Taft in 1912 issued an executive order prescribing the arrangement of the stars on the union, there was neither uniformity of custom nor any legal regulation in that regard. How can it be pretended, then, that because the stars are now established in horizontal rows (six rows in 1912, seven in 1959, and nine in 1960), they were thus arranged from the beginning of United States history? And since such was not the case, how can any State lay claim to any particular star?

Sufficient refutation of this sentimental fancy is supplied by these simple facts: the stars were in the flag for more than a decade before the Constitution was adopted; the thirteen original States were never "admitted" to the Union, and thus have no differing order of admission; the five States admitted following 1794 had no stars at all until July 4, 1818, when the Third Flag Act became effective; until 1912 there was no legal order of arrangement of the stars on the union; and finally, during the debates over adoption of the Flag Act of 1818, the idea of identifying each State with a particular star was proposed but definitely rejected. The stars thus represent the States collectively, and no particular star has any regional or local significance.[11]

CHAPTER 13 ★

The Flag Today

WHEN ON JULY 4, 1776, THE CONTINENTAL CONgress enacted the Declaration of Independence, the newborn nation consisted of thirteen feeble States having a total population of less than three million people. Today the United States of America has become the most powerful country in the free world, with a sea-to-sea population more than sixty times greater than in Revolutionary War days, and with important possessions and responsibilities all over the globe. The Stars and Stripes authorized on June 14, 1777, has likewise undergone impressive growth, and now has fifty stars in its union instead of the original thirteen. More significant even than this, the flag has become hallowed by a wealth of patriotic sacrifices and associations.

In 1912 New Mexico and Arizona were admitted to the Union, increasing the number of States to forty-eight. Keeping step with this development, President Taft issued an executive order on June 24, 1912, in which the relative proportions of the flag and the arrangement of the stars were officially prescribed, investigation having disclosed that no less than sixty-six different sizes and proportions were currently in use by the several executive departments of the Federal Government. Henceforth there would be only twelve different sizes, having uniform proportions of design.[1]

The forty-eight-star flag thus created (Pl. XXI-47) remained our national emblem for more than forty-six years and was carried by the armed forces of the United States in two great World Wars. Then on January 3, 1959, following the admission of Alaska as the forty-ninth State, President Eisenhower issued Executive Order No. 10798 establishing a new Stars and Stripes with a union having seven stars in each of seven rows (Pl. XXI-48). This went into official effect on July 4 of that year, when at 12:01 A.M. the new flag was hoisted with impressive ceremonies over the ramparts of old Fort McHenry, at Baltimore, Maryland. The flagstaff used for this purpose was a newly constructed replica of the 1814 flagpole from which flew the emblem that inspired Francis Scott Key to write "The Star-Spangled Banner." Included in the ceremonies was a re-enactment of the British bombardment by United States naval vessels and units of the United States Army 1st Artillery.[2]

Alaska did not long enjoy the distinction of being the last State to be represented on the flag. Within a few short months Hawaii, also, was admitted to Statehood. This called for a new design and arrangement of stars in the union, a requirement met by President Eisenhower in Executive Order No. 10834, issued August 21, 1959. To conform with this, a national banner with fifty stars became "the official flag of the United States" on July 4, 1960 (Pl. XXI-49).[3]

It remains only to describe this newest and latest Stars and Stripes. By the provisions of Executive Order No. 10834, Part I, its design is specifically established in these words:

SECTION 1. The flag of the United States shall have thirteen horizontal stripes, alternate red and white, and a union consisting of white stars on a field of blue.

SEC. 2. The positions of the stars in the union of the flag and in the union jack shall be as indicated on the attachment to this order, which is hereby made a part of this order.

SEC. 3. The dimensions of the constituent parts of the flag shall conform to the proportions set forth in the attachment referred to in section 2 of this order.

The attachment mentioned in this direct quotation is in two parts. The first of these is a scale drawing of the new flag, showing seven red and six white stripes of equal width, and a union with fifty five-pointed white stars in nine rows, so arranged that there are six stars in each of five alternate rows starting from the top, and five stars in each of the four intervening rows.

The second part of the attachment is a table establishing "Standard Proportions" of the flag, regardless of variations in overall size. Taking the hoist or width of the flag as 1, these are as follows:

Hoist (width) of flag .... 1.
Fly (length) of flag 1.9

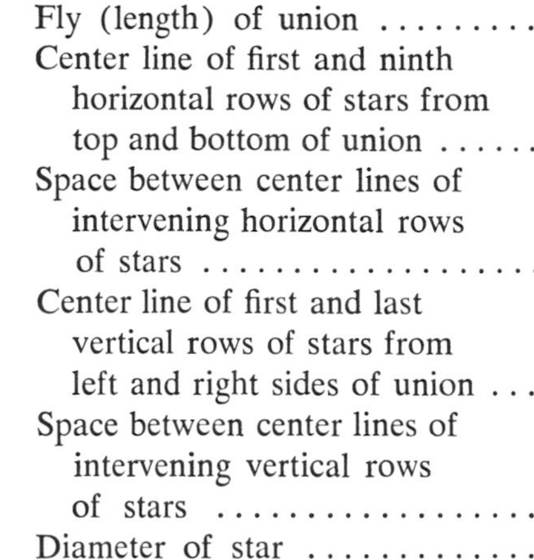

Hoist (width) of union .... .5385 (7/13)
Fly (length) of union .... .76
Center line of first and ninth horizontal rows of stars from top and bottom of union ...... .054
Space between center lines of intervening horizontal rows of stars .... .054
Center line of first and last vertical rows of stars from left and right sides of union ... .063
Space between center lines of intervening vertical rows of stars .... .063
Diameter of star .... .0616
Width of stripe .... .0769 (1/13)

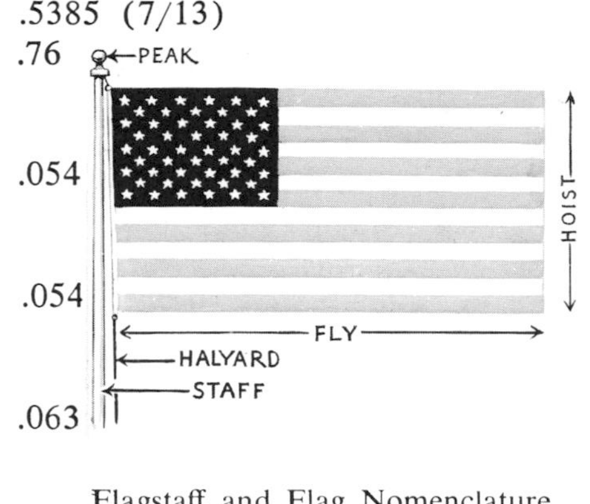

Flagstaff and Flag Nomenclature

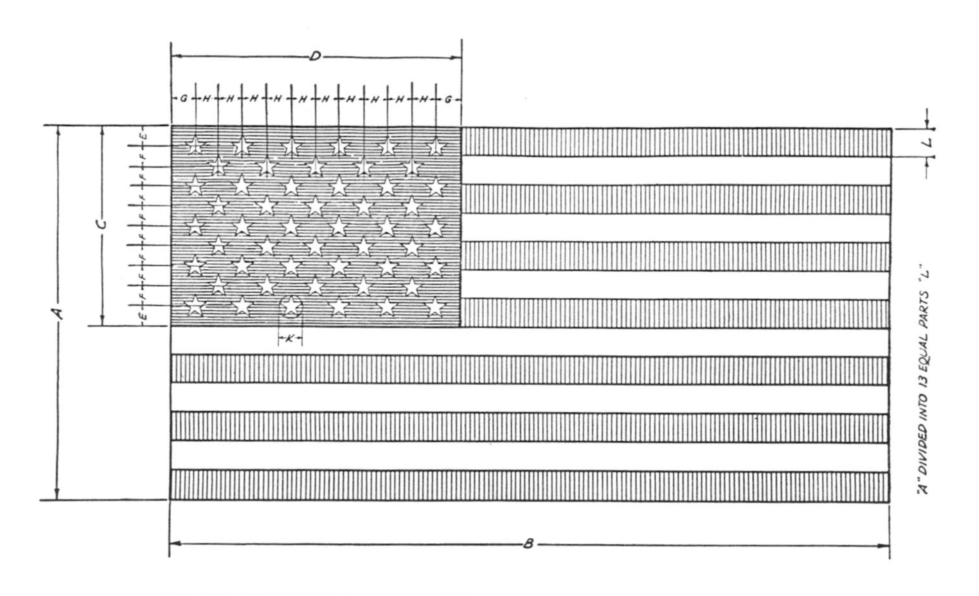

STANDARD PROPORTIONS									
HOIST (WIDTH) OF FLAG	FLY (LENGTH) OF FLAG	HOIST (WIDTH) OF UNION	FLY (LENGTH) OF UNION					DIAMETER OF STAR	WIDTH OF STRIPE
1.	1.9	.5385 (7/13)	.76	.054	.054	.063	.063	.0616	.0769 (1/13)
A	B	C	D	E	F	G	H	K	L

Design Specifications of the 50-Star Flag

Part II of Executive Order No. 10834 has numerous provisions, but only a few are pertinent for discussion here. Section 21 fixes eleven sizes of flags for executive departments and independent establishments of the Federal Government, including wholly-owned Government corporations. The largest of these is twenty feet in hoist and thirty-eight feet in fly, the smallest one and thirty-two hundredths feet in hoist and two and one-half feet in fly. Section 23 provides that exterior dimensions of each union jack "shall equal the respective exterior dimensions of the union of a flag of a size authorized or pursuant" to the order, and further states that the "size of the union jack flown with the national flag shall be the same as the size of the union of that national flag." And finally, by Section 24, the Secretary of Defense and the Administrator of General Services are given the right, for cause deemed sufficient by them, to "make minor adjustments in one or more of the dimensions or proportionate dimensions prescribed" by the order, or to "authorize proportions or sizes other than those prescribed."[4]

This is the Stars and Stripes today. Born almost casually and with vagueness of design in 1777, its antecedents reach back to the national flags of Great Britian and thence to those of other lands. Comparatively unimportant and limited in use at first, associated in its early history with much confusion and contradiction, and veiled at times in spurious myth and legend, it has gradually become with the passing years an ever more fixed and secure symbol of the nation. Through foreign war and great civil conflict it has endured, and in enduring has spread United States influence from the thirteen original States of the Atlantic seaboard to the Mississippi Valley, across the plains of Texas, on to Oregon and California, and thence to Alaska and the tropical waters of the mid-Pacific. More than a million people have sacrificed and given their life blood in its defense, and for Americans it has come to signify honor and love of country beyond price. May it wave proudly forever, this Stars and Stripes, a glorious, living symbol of human dignity, liberty under law, and equal opportunity for fulfillment of men's hopes!

Part II

ADDITIONAL SYMBOLS OF UNITED STATES SOVEREIGNTY

CHAPTER 14 ★

The Seal of the United States

THE GREAT SEAL OR THE SEAL OF THE UNITED STATES (Pl. XXII-50 and 51), as it is variously known, symbolizes American sovereignty. Its origin goes back to the Revolutionary War and our struggle to achieve independent national status. The seal is impressed upon many state documents, thereby certifying and authenticating official acts of the Federal Government.

There are two sides to the seal, obverse and reverse. Most Americans daily handle a piece of paper that carries facsimiles of both sides. Very few people realize that on the green back of a one-dollar bill both sides of the Great Seal of the United States are pictured.

The obverse side by itself has been used extensively and is recognized as the Seal of the United States. Except for its appearance on the one-dollar bill, and its occasional use as an illustration, people rarely see the design of the reverse side.

The obverse side is at the right on the green back of the one-dollar bill. Its central feature is the American eagle with a cluster of thirteen stars over its head. On the eagle's breast may be seen a shield representing the Union of the thirteen original States and the Congress. The eagle's right talon holds an olive branch; its left talon, a bundle of arrows. According to the authors of the design, these two features represent the powers of peace and war, respectively. In its beak the eagle holds a streamer bearing the motto "E Pluribus Unum." Translated from the Latin, this means "Out of Many, One."

The central part of the reverse side design is an unfinished pyramid. It represents strength and duration. Over the pyramid is the "eye of Providence" placed in a triangle. Above the eye are the Latin words "Annuit Coeptis." Translated, this means "He has favored our undertaking." The Latin words beneath the pyramid, "Novus Ordo Seclorum," signify "A New Order of the Ages."

With the signing of the Declaration of Independence on July 4, 1776, it became important to obtain a usable symbol of sovereignty for the newly established nation. On that same date the Continental Congress adopted a resolution stating "that Dr. Franklin, Dr. J. Adams, and Mr. Jefferson be a committee, to bring in a device for a Seal for the United States of America." This committee of distinguished men reported to Congress in August, 1776, suggesting Biblical subjects for the seal design. Congress tabled its report. A new committee restudied the subject in March, 1780, including a review of the report submitted by its predecessor, but accomplished nothing.

PLATE XVII *38*

The first regimental flag of the United States Army and used as the National Color of the Army, probably from 1787 to 1791. The original of this flag is in the custody of Trinity Church, New York City, and is displayed in the Chapel of Saint Cornelius on Governor's Island in New York Harbor, headquarters of the United States First Army. The flag is 8 by 6 feet, 6 inches, and is made of dark blue silk. The eagle, shown in flight above a base of white clouds with a huge sunburst around it capped by 13 seven-pointed stars, holds a sheaf of 7 arrows in one talon and an olive branch in the other. At the end of the American Revolution the army was mustered out of existence. In 1787 the Congress established an armed force of one regiment that constituted the Army of the United States after the adoption of the Constitution in 1789. Not until 1834 was the Army given the right to carry the Stars and Stripes. Until then each organization, company or regiment, carried a flag of its own design. Existing records of Trinity Church do not disclose how or when this flag came into its possession. An undocumented tradition alleges that General Lafayette designed the flag and presented it to General George Washington during the Revolution.

39

The United States 1st Infantry Regiment National Color, the oldest numbered United States national color in existence. There is a very close resemblance to the flag shown in No. 38, the principal difference being the designation "U.S. 1st Regt." in a wreath. This flag is in the West Point Museum Collections. It is 54¼ by 76½ inches in size and shows 13 stripes on the shield and 13 eight-pointed stars above the sunburst. This flag has cloth underneath it underpainted to recreate the eagle's head and part of one wing, which have been destroyed in the original. The Congress authorized the formation of the 2nd Regiment of Infantry in 1791 to protect the western frontier. At that time the earlier regiment established in 1787 became the 1st Regiment of Infantry and it is believed that this flag then (1791) became its National Color. The 1st Infantry Regiment of 1791 is now the 3rd Infantry Regiment. *Courtesy United States Military Academy, West Point, New York*

PLATE XVII

38

39

40
4th United States Infantry Regiment National Color, 1796-1812. The 4th Infantry was organized in 1796. A flag like this was captured by the British at Detroit in the War of 1812 and is at the Chelsea Royal Hospital, London.

41
National Color or "Standard" of the 1st Regiment of Light Artillery, 1808-1821. The original of this flag is in the West Point Museum Collections. It is 68 by 83 inches in size. There are 17 stripes on the shield and 17 five-pointed stars above the eagle, which holds 6 arrows in its talon. The Regiment of Light Artillery was organized in 1808 and this flag appears to have been used in the War of 1812. The flag is marked "First" since a 2nd Regiment was anticipated.

42
Standard of the 2nd Regiment of United States Cavalry. The original of this flag is in the West Point Museum Collections. It is 27 by 30 inches in size. There are 13 five-pointed stars above the eagle, which holds 7 arrows in its talon. The 2nd Dragoons, organized in 1836, became the 2nd Cavalry Regiment in 1861. The color of the cavalry standard did not change until 1887. This flag apparently dates from the Civil War period.

Yet a third committee was finally appointed in 1782 to obtain a design for the seal.

After consulting with Mr. William Barton, of Philadelphia, who was known to be an authority on the subject of heraldry, this third committee submitted its report in May, 1782. Congress still had reservations about the design, however, and on June 13 following turned over to Charles Thomson, its secretary, the entire collection of reports and designs prepared by all three committees. Thomson studied this material, adopted certain items from the different reports and designs, made a rough drawing in color of his own suggestion, and wrote a description to accompany it. This being finished, he presented his art work to Barton, who further revised the obverse side of the seal.

Barton changed Thomson's design, providing the thirteen vertical stripes alternately white and red below the rectangular blue field on the eagle's breast, and specifying that there should be thirteen arrows in the eagle's left talon. Explaining the symbolism of this shield, he pointed out that the white and red stripes represented the thirteen States supporting the blue field (a chief) which united the whole and represented Congress, and that the colors were taken from the American Flag. White signified purity and innocence; red, hardiness and valor; and blue, vigilance, perseverance, and justice.

Thomson received Barton's revision on June 19 and drew up a report to Congress. This used Barton's description of the latest design of the obverse side and his own earlier description of the reverse side, which had been based largely on Barton's earlier work. Thomson submitted his report on June 20, and Congress approved it the same day. The blazon of the Great Seal, the heraldic term for the detailed description of a coat of arms, in this way became part of the law of the land. The blazon, or description of the seal, as thus established, reads as follows:

ARMS. Paleways of thirteen pieces, argent and gules; a chief, azure; the escutcheon on the breast of the American eagle displayed proper, holding in his dexter talon an olive branch, and in his sinister a bundle of thirteen arrows, all proper, and in his beak a scroll, inscribed with the motto, *"E Pluribus Unum."*

For the CREST. Over the head of the eagle, which appears above the escutcheon, a glory, or, breaking through a cloud, proper, and surrounding thirteen stars, forming a constellation, argent, on an azure field.

REVERSE. A pyramid unfinished. In the zenith, an eye in a triangle, surrounded with a glory proper. Over the eye these words, *"Annuit Coeptis."* On the base of the pyramid the numerical letters MDCCLXXVI. And underneath the following motto, *"Novus Ordo Seclorum."*

During the first seven years of its use the seal was in custody of Charles Thomson, Secretary of Congress. Since September 15, 1789, the Secretary of State has been the custodian. Altogether, from 1782 to the present day, there have been seven dies cut of the seal's obverse side for use in authenticating state documents. The reverse side has never been used as a seal proper. Most people have considered it heavy, prosaic, and inappropriate.

The first die of the seal was cut in brass in 1782 and continued to be used as late as April, 1841. Its impress measured about 2¼ inches in diameter. It is easily indentifiable by several peculiarities. These include a border of modified acanthus leaves, six-pointed stars, and arrows touching the border. This die is now on permanent display at the National Archives, Washington, D.C.

In the early years of our nation's history, treaties called for a different type of impression than that of the first die cut in 1782. Usually, these were wax seals of large size attached to the papers by cords, conforming to procedures followed by European countries. Because of this, the Department of State in 1825 had a Washington, D.C., jeweler and silversmith make a special Great Seal. The resulting steel die measured 4 11/16 inches in diameter and 1¼ inches in thickness. Use of this special pendant seal was discontinued in 1871 by order of Secretary of State Hamilton Fish. Since then the regular die of the Great Seal has been used on treaties as well as on other state papers.

A special die of the 1825 seal was cut in 1854 for use in embossing the skippet (a metal box protecting the pendant wax seal that was attached by ornamental cords to treaties). There is one known instance of the use of this skippet, or cover, die on a treaty of commerce and navigation with Italy in 1871. With the discontinuance of the pendant seal in that year, the skippet-cover seal also went out of use in the United States.

In 1841 a cast steel die made in Washington replaced the first seal of 1782. Although about equal to the latter in size, it was distinguishable by its use of small five-pointed stars and a sheaf of six instead of thirteen arrows.

The fifth die was made in 1877 in Washington and resembled the die of 1841. Both the fourth and the fifth dies ignored the law passed by Congress in 1782, in that neither one had thirteen arrows in the eagle's left talon.

Because they did not comply with the basic legislation establishing the Seal of the United States, as noted above, the 1841 and 1877 dies were criticized. In 1882, therefore, the Secretary of State asked Congress for an appropriation of $1,000 for the purpose of making a new seal. This request was granted on July 7, 1884, and pursuant to the act of Congress passed on that date, Tiffany and Company, of New York City, cut a new obverse die in 1885. This was three inches in diameter and adhered strictly to the description of the blazon in the law of 1782. There is reason to believe that Tiffany also cut a reverse die of the Great Seal at the same time, but this has never been found, and if made was apparently never used.

In 1902 Congress appropriated $1,250 for a new die because the sixth was wearing down to the point where it made poor impressions. The Department of State decided that the new die should reproduce the previous design as exactly as possible, thus complying faithfully with the law of 1782. Bailey, Banks & Little, a Philadelphia firm, cut this seventh die in hardened steel, and it is the one used today for affixing seals on state papers. The seal is now invariably impressed upon a paper wafer which is in turn affixed to the document with paste.

Thus, altogether, there have been seven dies of the obverse side of the Great Seal of the United States cut and used in the course of our history. Only the sixth and seventh of these represent the precise design and arrangement as seen today, and as illustrated in this book. Many of the earlier dies are in the permanent exhibit about the seal which has been installed on the north mezzanine of the main State Department Building in Washington, D.C.

Today the seal is placed on the following types of papers and documents after they have been signed by the President and countersigned by the Secretary of State:

Presidential proclamations
Ratification of treaties
Papers granting powers to individuals named to negotiate and sign treaties or similar types of agreements
Documents of recognition issued to consular officers on the basis of commissions issued by foreign appointing governments (This is called *Exequator*.)

Presidential warrants for the extradition of fugitives from the justice of the United States

Commissions of all Cabinet officers, ambassadors, ministers, and other Foreign Service officials

All other civil officers appointed by the President and whose commissions are not issued under some other seal as required by law

Envelopes to contain letters of recall and credence and other communications from the President to the heads of foreign governments

Growth and volume of official business since the seal was first used have made it necessary to modify the number and kinds of documents to which it is applied. The basic law governing such use is a Congressional Act of September 15, 1789. This changed the Department of Foreign Affairs to the Department of State, gave custody of the seal to the Secretary of State, and required that the seal be affixed as follows:

> . . . to all civil commissions, for officers of the United States, to be appointed by the President by and with the advice and consent of the Senate, or by the President alone. *Provided,* that the said seal shall not be affixed to any commission, before the same shall have been signed by the President of the United States, nor to any other instrument or act, without the special warrant of the President therefor.

With the lapse of time and the growth of the Government, it became impractical to have all civil commissions signed by the President impressed with the seal. Presidential appointees who now serve under Cabinet officers other than the Secretary of State are commissioned under the seals of their respective departments. In 1952, also, an executive order authorized and instructed the Secretary of State to affix the seal to documents in a series of listed categories without special warrant signed by the President.

The seal has two correct designations in general usage as well as in law. These are: (1) The Great Seal, and (2) The Seal of the United States. Both terms are found in Acts of Congress and in a Supreme Court decision. The resolution of Congress passed June 20, 1782, creating the seal, referred to it as "The Great Seal." There seems to be a rather long-standing preference, however, in official circles, for the term "The Seal of the United States."

As a matter of historical interest, the earliest known document bearing the Seal of the United States is dated September 16, 1782. It is a grant of full authority and power to General George Washington to arrange with the British for the exchange, subsistence, and better treatment of prisoners of war.

We have already mentioned that both sides of the seal are reproduced on the green back side of the one-dollar bill. The obverse side is used as a decoration in many other ways. It appears as a brass decoration on all Army and Air Force officers' service caps. Its design also decorates American soldiers' uniform buttons. It appears on State Department stationery, and very frequently is found on medals, currency, publications, flags, and monuments. With an added outside encircling legend, "Department of State United States of America," it is used as the State Department seal. The design is found in large size and often in color above the entrances to American embassies, legations, and consulates throughout the world. In small size it is used on the seal of all United States Foreign Service establishments.

Use of the seal design in decorations, commercial or otherwise, official or unofficial, has never been regulated by law. In the early days of the Republic it often decorated the headboard of a bed, a chest, a chair back, a set of china, wallpaper, or even a butter mold. In more recent years, American sentiment seems to be supporting the State Department's view that a facsimile of the Seal of the United States is inappropriate for decoration of commercial items. Its use in that manner appears to be declining.

CHAPTER 15 ★

The Coat of Arms, Seal, and Flag of the President of the United States

THE THREE SYMBOLS AND EMBLEMS OF THE PRESIdent's authority are his coat of arms, his seal, and his flag (Pl. XXII-52 and 53). Except as changes are required when new States are admitted to the Union, these remain more or less constant from one President to another. All three symbols have a common basic design, with the coat of arms forming part of both the seal and the flag. Each derives its present form from an executive order issued by President Truman on October 25, 1945, since slightly modified by the executive orders of May 26, 1959, and February 5, 1960, issued by President Eisenhower. These modifications provided for the addition of a forty-ninth star for Alaska and a fiftieth star for Hawaii, effective July 4, 1959, and July 4, 1960, respectively.

THE PRESIDENT'S COAT OF ARMS

A President's coat of arms has been in use since 1880, when one was first used by President Hayes. It had no legal definition, however, until President Truman's executive order of 1945. The coat of arms used from 1880 to 1945 violated heraldic custom in one respect: the eagle faced toward its own left. Unless otherwise described in the heraldic notice, the eagle on a coat of arms always faces toward its own right. How the error developed in the case of the President's seal is unknown, but it was not corrected until 1945. At that time Mr. Arthur E. DuBois, Chief of the Heraldic Section, Office of the Quartermaster General of the Army, altered the design so as to have the eagle's head turned toward its own right, which is the direction of honor. In this way the eagle also faces the olive branch of peace held in its right (dexter) talon, rather than the bundle of arrows in its left (sinister) talon, symbolic of war. Further details concerning the role played by Mr. DuBois in bringing about this change are given in the discussion below on the subject of the President's flag.

Under the executive order issued by President Truman in 1945, the President's coat of arms included a circle of forty-eight stars collectively representing the States then in the Union. No star denoted any particular State. The idea was that new stars would be added to the coat of arms, as additional States were admitted, at the same time as they were added to the Flag of the United States. The most recent executive order on the subject, No. 10860, issued by President Eisenhower on February 5, 1960, is here quoted in full, as follows:

Coat of Arms, Seal, and Flag of the President of the United States

By virtue of the authority vested in me as President of the United States, it is hereby ordered as follows:

Section 1. The Coat of Arms of the President of the United States shall be of the following design:

SHIELD: Paleways of thirteen pieces argent and gules, a chief azure; upon the breast of an American eagle displayed holding in his dexter talon an olive branch and in his sinister a bundle of thirteen arrows all proper, and in his beak a white scroll inscribed "E PLURIBUS UNUM" sable.

CREST: Behind and above the eagle a radiating glory or, on which appears an arc of thirteen cloud puffs proper, and a constellation of thirteen mullets argent.

The whole surrounded by white stars arranged in the form of an annulet with one point of each star outward on the imaginary radiating center lines, the number of stars conforming to the number of stars in the union of the Flag of the United States as established by chapter 1 of title 4 of the United States Code.

Sec. 2. The Seal of the President of the United States shall consist of the Coat of Arms encircled by the words "Seal of the President of the United States."

Sec. 3. The Color and Flag of the President of the United States shall consist of a dark blue rectangular background of sizes and proportions to conform to military and naval custom, on which shall appear the Coat of Arms of the President in proper colors. The proportions of the elements of the Coat of Arms shall be in direct relation to the hoist, and the fly shall vary according to the customs of the military and naval services.

Sec. 4. The Coat of Arms, Seal, and Color and Flag shall be as described herein and as set forth in the illustrations and specifications which accompany this order and which are hereby made a part thereof. These designs shall be used to represent the President of the United States exclusively.

Sec. 5. This order shall become effective on July 4, 1960, and Executive Order No. 10823 of May 26, 1959, shall be superseded as of that date.

DWIGHT D. EISENHOWER

THE WHITE HOUSE
February 5, 1960

THE PRESIDENT'S SEAL

The President's seal, like the President's coat of arms, has been a part of our history since 1880, when it also was first used by President Hayes. Again like the coat of arms, it had no legal definition until one was provided by President Truman's executive order of 1945. In this document, as already noted above, the design was changed, under the influence of Mr. Arthur E. DuBois, so that the eagle faced toward its own right. President Truman also decided that the eagle on his seal and his flag should be in the colors of the natural bird, rather than in white as it had appeared on the former President's flag. As indicated both in his executive order and those subsequently issued by President Eisenhower, the seal is identical with the coat of arms, except that it is surrounded with the words "Seal of the President of the United States" incorporated in an outer circle.

THE PRESIDENT'S FLAG

The first President's flag dates from 1916, when one was adopted by President Wilson. Prior to that time, there were different flags (the Army and the Navy each had one) for the President. Deciding that it would be desirable to have one standard Presidential flag, President Wilson asked the Assistant Secretary of the Navy, Franklin

43

Charles Willson Peale portrait of Washington at the battle of Trenton showing an American flag in upper right background. Peale painted a portrait of Washington from life at Princeton in 1779. Subsequently he made several copies of it, at least four, up to and through 1781. This copy, which he made prior to August, 1780, came down from the Washington family. Its flag shows 13 white, six-pointed stars in a circle on a field of blue. There are no red and white stripes. The painting shows background scenery of the Trenton battlefield rather than that of Princeton, which is shown in the original life portrait of 1779. *Courtesy Metropolitan Museum of Art, Gift of Collis P. Huntington, 1896*

44
Popular or Betsy Ross Version of the United States Flag, Revolutionary War Period

45

46

D. Roosevelt, and Commodore Byron McCandless, USN, Aide to the Secretary of the Navy, to design a suitable emblem. On May 29, 1916, President Wilson signed an executive order adopting a design recommended by them. This design carried the President's coat of arms on a blue field with a white star in each of the four corners. The President's flag thus established remained in use until superseded by the new one specified in President Truman's executive order of October 25, 1945.

In March, 1945, President Franklin D. Roosevelt decided it was inappropriate for the President's flag to have only four stars, whereas those of Fleet Admiral and General of the Army (grades established in December, 1944) had five stars each. He first discussed the matter with his naval aide, Vice Admiral Wilson Brown, and then, remem-

---

PLATE XX *45*

Fort Sumter 33-star Flag (Garrison Flag). There were two flags at Fort Sumter in April, 1861, when the Confederates opened fire on the fort: the larger, known as the Garrison Flag, and the smaller, the Post Flag (not a storm flag as often stated). The best evidence indicates that the Garrison Flag was flying over the fort at the time of the bombardment, April 12-13, 1861. Maj. Robert L. Anderson (later general) saved the flags, and upon his arrival in Washington with them, following the surrender of the fort, they were officially presented to him. He kept possession of them until his death and they were preserved by his widow until her death on February 25, 1905. Mrs. Anderson's will provided that the flags should be given to the War Department for safekeeping. Secretary of War William Howard Taft on March 26, 1905, accepted the flags. They were wrapped and displayed in glass cases in the War Department. In both flags the union is in a fair state of preservation, but the remainder is badly tattered and torn and large parts are missing. Both Fort Sumter flags were transferred in 1955 from the Department of the Army to the National Park Service of the Department of Interior. They are now on display at Fort Sumter National Monument, Charleston, South Carolina. *Courtesy Fort Sumter National Monument, National Park Service*

46

Civil War 35-Star Flag. When the Civil War began the 33-star flag was the flag of the nation, although the admission of Kansas on January 29, 1861, as the 34th State made the 34-star flag official after July 4 of that year. During the war two more States were admitted —West Virginia on June 20, 1863, and Nevada on October 31, 1864 —thus making 36 States in the Union before the end of the war. The 35-star flag was flown during the last two years of the War, probably longer and more extensively than any other one during the Civil War.

bering his work with McCandless in 1916, turned to the latter for help in designing a new President's flag. Several designs based upon earlier American flags were accordingly prepared by Commodore McCandless, but they did not arrive in Washington until after the death of President Roosevelt.

President Truman first saw these McCandless flag designs in June, 1945, when he and members of his staff examined them carefully. He made several suggestions, including one that the flag ought to have a star for each State in the Union, and asked Commodore McCandless to submit a new design with a circle of forty-eight stars around the coat of arms. McCandless prepared a design accordingly and sent it to Washington in July, 1945, but the President was unable to see this until he returned from the Potsdam Conference in August. He then gave it his tentative approval, but passed the design on to the War and Navy Departments for comments and suggestions.

It was during the course of this review that Mr. Arthur E. DuBois, then Chief of the Heraldic Section, Office of the Quartermaster General of the Army, made several suggestions to President Truman about the proposed design. He pointed out that the flag suggested, reproducing the President's seal and coat of arms in use since 1880, was apparently based upon an erroneous rendering of the Great Seal of the United States, in that the eagle faced toward its left (sinister) talon, whereas on the Great Seal the eagle faced toward its right (dexter) talon. Mr. DuBois further observed that according to heraldic custom, unless otherwise specified in the heraldic description, an eagle on a coat of arms should always properly face toward its own right. Thus the design of the Great Seal of the United States was correct, that of the President's coat of arms incorrect. President Truman then asked Mr. DuBois to redesign the coat of arms, seal, and flag in accord with heraldic custom and the Great Seal of the United States. He also decided at this time that the eagle on the President's seal and the President's flag should appear in full color, and not in white, as it had on the former President's flag.

In the President's flag, as in the coat of arms and the seal symbolizing his authority, the stars in a surrounding circle represent the States collectively, no star denoting any particular State. As additional States are admitted to the Union, new stars will be added to the President's coat of arms, seal, and flag at the same time that such stars are added to the Flag of the United States. All three emblems thus had forty-eight stars in the surrounding circle in 1945, and another star was added when the forty-nine-star Flag of the United States became effective on July 4, 1959. When the new fifty-star flag replaced the latter as our national standard on July 4, 1960, the President's coat of arms, seal, and flag were changed accordingly to have fifty stars in the surrounding circle.

The colors used in the President's flag have been most recently described in Executive Order No. 10860, issued by President Eisenhower on February 5, 1960, and already quoted in the discussion above about the President's coat of arms. As given in that document, the colors are as follows:

Specifications for President's Flag

Flag base—blue.
Stars, large and small—white.
Shield:
  Chief—light blue.
  Stripes—white and red.
Eagle:
  Wings, body, upper legs—shades of brown.
  Head, neck, tail—white, shaded gray.
  Beak, feet, lower legs—yellow.
  Talons—dark gray, white high lights.
Arrows—white shaded gray.
Olive branch:
  Leaves, stem—shades of green.
  Olives—light green.
Rays—yellow.
Clouds—white, shaded gray.
Scroll—white with gray shadows.
Letters—black.
All dimensions are exclusive of heading and hems.
Device to appear on both sides of flag but will appear reversed on reverse side of flag, except that the motto shall read from left to right on both sides.

Also part of Executive Order No. 10860 is a scale drawing of the design of the President's flag in black and white. Accompanying this is a table showing the relative proportions of every feature of the design to the hoist, except that no relative dimension is given for the fly, or length, of the flag. However, as stated in Section 3 of the order, the dark blue background of the President's flag, which of course determines its overall dimensions, is to be of "sizes and proportions to conform to military and naval custom."

Part III

OTHER FLAGS THAT HAVE REPRESENTED NATIONAL SOVEREIGNTY IN THE UNITED STATES

CHAPTER 16 ★

The Lone Star Flag of Texas

"GIVE US A FLAG TO FIGHT UNDER . . . IN TIME TO hoist it in defiance of Santa Anna." This was Colonel James W. Fannin's plea to the provisional government of Texas in February, 1836, during the territory's short but savage struggle for independence from Mexico. Fannin did not live to see an official Texas flag. In March following he and his command were captured and executed by order of Mexican General Santa Anna.

Early in March, 1836, the Texas Constitutional Convention appointed a committee to design a flag for the young Republic, and on the 11th of that month accepted a design by Lorenzo de Zavala, a member of the committee. Little is known about this design except that a rainbow and two stars were added on the following day. Neither is there any evidence that the proposed flag was ever made. The threat of Mexican attack put the convention to flight, and for several weeks the fate of Texas hung in the balance, until Sam Houston's small and outnumbered army won its stunning victory at San Jacinto on April 21, 1836.

Eight months after independence was achieved, the first Texas Congress, on December 10, 1836, adopted a new flag for the Republic. This standard, probably designed by David G. Burnet, provisional president of Texas during the Revolution, consisted of a single gold star set against an azure background. This "lone star" design was already a popular one in Texas. Many of the volunteer units which came from the United States to fight for Texas independence carried flags emblazoned with a star, probably as a sentimental link with the stars on their own national emblem. Even before the declaration of independence from Mexico, Stephen F. Austin, the

"Father of Texas," had proposed a national flag which included a star, symbolic of the Republic-to-be. Because of unsettled conditions in Texas and lack of facilities for communicating such information to its scattered settlements, the Burnet flag never became widely known or used.

On January 25, 1839, President Mirabeau B. Lamar approved an act of the Third Texas Congress which specified the design of a new national flag. This was the famous Lone Star Flag (Pl. XXIII-54), which serves today as the State's official banner. Traditionally credited as its designer is Dr. Charles B. Stewart, a prominent figure in the Republic's early days. The law provided that the Texas flag should consist of a blue perpendicular stripe of width equal to one-third the length of the fly, with a white five-pointed star in the center; and one red and one white horizontal stripe of equal width, the white stripe uppermost, completing the remaining two-thirds of the flag's length. This Lone Star Flag represented the young nation for seven years, until Texas was annexed to the United States on December 29, 1845. Even then it continued to fly over the capital at Austin until February 19, 1846, when the last President of the Republic, Anson Jones, handed over executive leadership to the newly-elected Governor, J. Pinckney Henderson. With the admission of Texas there were twenty-eight stars in the United States Flag.

When Texas seceded from the Union in February, 1861, the Lone Star Flag once more became the asserted sovereign standard of the State, retaining that distinction until the Stars and Bars of the Confederate States of America replaced it on March 4 following. With the end of the Civil War in 1865, the Flag of the United States was again raised over Texas.

The original description of the Lone Star Flag as given in the act of January 25, 1839, was clarified by the Texas legislature in 1933. No changes were made in the flag, but the new law specified that the single star, from its topmost to lowest points, should be approximately one-third the depth of the blue field. A code for Texas flag usage was adopted at the same time.

PLATE XXI

47
United States 48-Star Flag, 1913-1959

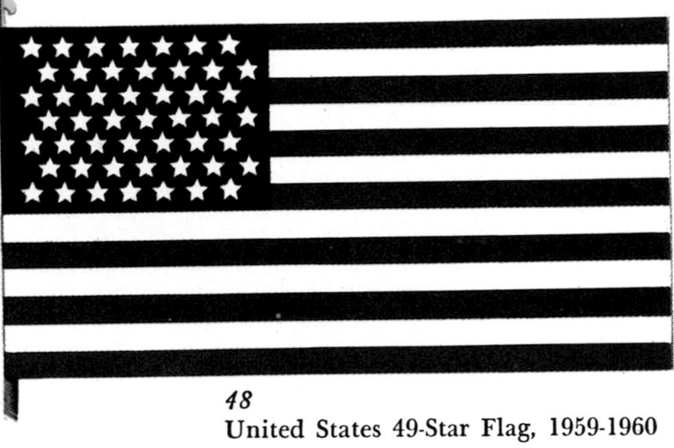

48
United States 49-Star Flag, 1959-1960

49
United States 50-Star Flag, 1960

Plate XXII

50
Great Seal of the United States (Obverse)

51
Great Seal of the United States (Reverse)

52
The President's Seal

53
The President's Flag.

CHAPTER 17 ★

The California Bear Flag

IN THE SPRING OF 1846 THE MEXICAN PROVINCE OF Alta California was ripe for revolution. About a thousand "foreigners"—settlers of American or European extraction—lived among its ten thousand inhabitants of Spanish or Mexican descent. Three quarters of these were from the United States, and most of them were concentrated about San Francisco Bay and in the Sacramento Valley.

Nearly all these foreigners looked forward to the prosperity which they believed would come to California under a new government. To the Americans this change meant nothing less than incorporating the province into the Union, or, failing that, establishing an independent republic. The more conservative settlers hoped that such a shift could be accomplished peacefully and with the co-operation of their friends the Californians. Many others, however, were people with little property who had scant sympathy for the Mexicans. They wanted either immediate annexation or the establishment of an independent state by force.

By March, 1846, it seemed to many foreigners that the moment for action had arrived. Brevet Captain John C. Frémont, of the United States Topographical Engineers, had entered California on an exploring expedition without permission of the Mexican authorities. Approaching Monterey with his force of about sixty armed men, he was ordered by the alarmed officials to leave at once. Frémont "peremptorily refused" and fortified himself on nearby Gavilán Peak. American settlers throughout northern California prepared to rush to his aid, but a note from the United States consul induced the explorer to remember that fighting was no part of his mission. Frémont then retired northward, intending to return home by way of Oregon.

Deprived of their excuse, and not feeling strong enough to challenge the Mexican authority on their own, the settlers remained at their homes.

April and May of 1846 were uneasy months for many of the foreigners in northern California. They knew that war between the United States and Mexico might break out at any time. Tension increased when the California authorities, emboldened by their success in "driving out" Frémont, began reiterating oft-repeated and empty threats to expel the settlers, most of whom were in the country without required passports. The ranking military officer in the province, Comandante General José Castro, with headquarters at Monterey, set about raising troops to overthrow his arch rival, Governor Pío Pico, whose seat of government was in Los Angeles. As a cover-up for his military preparations in this regard, he issued warnings against the foreign peril.

Little wonder, then, that some of the settlers came to feel themselves "threatened" and that they flocked to Frémont's camp when he returned to the Sacremento Valley from Oregon after being overtaken by Lieutenant Archibald H. Gillespie of the United States Marine Corps. Although Frémont had no orders to stir up a revolt among the settlers, he advised them to organize for their own defense.

Early in June, 1846, General Castro visited San Rafael, on the northern shore of San Francisco Bay. There he obtained a herd of horses which he dispatched under escort to his headquarters by way of the Sacramento Valley. Believing these animals were intended for use against the foreigners, a group of eleven or twelve settlers at Frémont's camp on Feather River determined to seize them. Led by a grizzled mountain man named Ezekiel Merritt, they surprised the escort on the Consumnes River on June 10. The Californians were permitted to continue their journey, but the mounts were taken to Frémont's camp.

The break was now made, and the settlers pushed their movement forward. At daybreak on June 14, 1846, Merritt's company, now grown to thirty-three or thirty-four men, captured the hamlet of Sonoma, north of San Francisco Bay. The town was ungarrisoned, but it contained a store of Mexican arms and the headquarters of M. G. Vallejo, commander of the northern frontier. Vallejo, two of his officers, and his American brother-in-law were sent as prisoners to Sutter's Fort.

On that same day William B. Ide was elected head of the "republican party," as the settlers now styled themselves. Needing an emblem for their cause, the men hunted about for materials from which to make a flag. Some white cotton was obtained for the field, and along its bottom edge was sewn a four-inch-wide strip of red flannel. A young man named William L. Todd, cousin to Mary Todd Lincoln, drew on its field designs suggested by the company. First came that traditional American emblem of independent Statehood, a single star, reminiscent of the Lone Star of Texas. Todd colored it in with red paint made (according to the best available contemporary description) from "blackberry juice, brick dust, & oil." Facing the star he also painted in red a crude representation of a grizzly bear standing on all fours. Beneath the star and the bear were outlined in black the words CALIFORNIA REPUBLIC. The completed flag, measuring thirty-six and one-half inches in hoist and fifty-nine inches in fly, evidently was raised on the Mexican flagstaff in front of the Sonoma barracks on June 14, 1846 (Pl. XXIII-55).

General Castro determined to crush the rebellion and soon had an advance unit of his army moving toward Sonoma. Hearing of this approaching force, the Bears, as the rebels soon became known, called upon Frémont for help. This appeal reached him about the same time as rumors that the Californians were planning to attack his camp. Believing he was duty-bound to protect his countrymen and his own honor, Frémont hurried to the relief of Sonoma. He arrived there on June 25, only to find that the settlers had already met Castro's advance force near San Rafael and routed it. Hoping to trap the enemy on the Marin Peninsula, he then dashed westward, but the Californians escaped by a clever ruse and retreated across the bay.

On July 5, 1846, Frémont assumed command of the revolt and reorganized the settler forces, which by that date numbered some 250 men. The next day he set out for Santa Clara, determined to whip Castro. Reaching Sutter's Fort, he learned on July 10 that the Mexican War had begun and that the United States Navy had raised the American Flag over Monterey. At Sonoma the Bear Flag had already been replaced the day before by the Stars and Stripes, brought by an officer from the U.S.S. *Portsmouth*. The Bears cheerfully dropped the idea of independence and joined the force raised by the Navy for the conquest of California. The "Republic of California" thus terminated its short existence.

The original Bear Flag was taken East by Commander John B.

Montgomery of the *Portsmouth* and deposited in the Boston Navy Yard along with other souvenirs of the Mexican War. In 1858 it was returned to San Francisco, remaining there in care of the Society of California Pioneers until destroyed during the fire of 1906. The official State flag of California, adopted by the State Legislature in 1911, is a refined adaptation of the banner hoisted at Sonoma on June 14, 1846.*

* Texas and California, the only States which attempted to win or actually achieved independence from a foreign power prior to joining the Union, are the only States with recognized claims to having had a national flag. (Hawaii, as we shall see in the next chapter, began as an independent kingdom.) Several Southern States, on seceding in 1861, asserted their independence; and some, like Louisiana, even produced a national flag of their own before joining the Confederacy. President Lincoln maintained, however, that none of the Southern States had actually been out of the Union, and this view was legally upheld by the United States Supreme Court in the decisive case of *Texas vs. White* in 1869.

CHAPTER 18 ★

The Flag of Hawaii

WHEN THE UNITED STATES FIFTY-STAR FLAG WENT up over Honolulu's Iolani Palace, the State capitol of Hawaii, on July 4, 1960, at its side was the Hawaii State Flag streaming out in the trade winds. While the fifty-star national flag has changed often in the course of its history, the Hawaii flag may have changed only once, and that inadvertently, in the course of its long history. It is the only flag representing any of the fifty states to have flown over a kingdom, a territory, a republic, and finally a state.

Its history reaches back almost to the days of Hawaii's earliest contact with Europeans. Its origin is not entirely clear and remains the subject of controversy among scholars of the subject.

The first certain and documented European contact with the Hawaiian Islands was in 1778 when Captain James Cook, the great British officer and explorer, landed at Waimea, Kauai, on January 18. He named the islands The Sandwich Islands, in honor of the Earl of Sandwich, the First Lord of the Admiralty. Captain Cook and his men were treated like gods by the natives, and it was with some reluctance that they left in the spring to search for the Northwest Passage. They returned to spend the following winter on the island of Hawaii, but this time trouble broke out with the natives who gradually discovered that their visitors were very human. In a fracas with the natives, while trying to recover a stolen boat, Cook was killed on February 14, 1779, at Kaawaloa, on the big island of Hawaii. A statue to him today marks the site.

By 1786 the islands had become a port of call for a few British and French ships. But it was not until Captain George Vancouver, who had first visited the islands with Captain Cook, made his three visits to

Hawaii in the 1790's that any European nation established a strong influence over the native rulers. On Vancouver's second and third visits, 1793 and 1794, he met all the important chiefs of the islands and went out of his way to avoid disturbances between his sailors and the natives. He especially tried to win the good will of Kamehameha, then a rising chieftain among several. During the period 1793-1794, Captain Vancouver established a British-Hawaii friendship and entente on a firm basis. Further, he obtained what he termed the "cession" of the islands to England on February 25, 1794, but the British Government apparently never took cognizance of it.

During his 1793 visit, Vancouver gave to Kamehameha a red ensign, or Union Jack, which at that date would have contained only the Cross of St. Andrew and the Cross of St. George. When Vancouver returned ten months later on his third visit he found the British ensign flying in front of Kamehameha's residence. Fifteen years later a traveler to Hawaii noticed the British flag had a place of honor in the King's home.

It appears that Kamehameha used this ensign as a flag on occasion, and it may very well have been his first flag, although an entirely unofficial one. Prior to this time, the Hawaiian chiefs carried cylinders of feathers as a symbol of distinction and other variously shaped standards, somewhat on the order of the standards of the Roman legions.

In the years before and immediately after 1800, Kamehameha the Great extended his sway over the Hawaiian Island group by conquest and established the Hawaiian kingdom. By 1810 he controlled all the islands except Kauai, which was protected by the wide, deep, and rough ocean passage that separated it from the other islands. During this time, if King Kamehameha used a flag at all it probably was the British Union Jack given to him in 1793 by Captain Vancouver.

The first recorded reference to a Hawaiian flag dates from the period immediately following the War of 1812. There are various accounts of the events that culminated in the designing of the first Hawaiian flag, but they all seem to agree substantially on the basic facts. During the war there was evidence in Hawaiian waters of the naval war between Great Britain and the United States. For instance, the British warship, *Cherub,* captured several American ships in Hawaiian waters.

One account states that an American privateer put into port and saw the British Union Jack flying. The captain sought an audience with King Kamehameha and asked for an explanation of why he was flying the enemy flag. King Kamehameha is said to have lowered the Union

Jack and raised the Stars and Stripes to satisfy the captain. A short time after the American privateer had departed a British ship arrived and its captain in turn demanded to know why the flag of his country's enemy was flying. King Kamehameha saw that he would be in constant trouble unless he found a solution to the flag problem. He called in some of his advisors. A proposal to fly both the British Union Jack and the American Stars and Stripes simultaneously was discarded. Out of the discussions came a decision to have a Hawaiian flag, which may have been intended to combine British and American flag characteristics.

The Russian navigator and explorer, Vasili Golovnin, who had served in the British navy under Nelson, circumnavigated the globe for the second time in 1817-1819 in the Russian corvette, *Kamchatka.* In 1818 he visited Hawaii and in his memoirs has given his understanding of how the Hawaiian flag originated. Golovnin wrote:

> He [Kamehameha I] took the English flag from Vancouver and used to hoist it always without knowing what it meant according to European standards. However, when during the last Anglo-American war one of the American captains said to him jokingly that the Americans have the right to take his islands away from him because he is flying the flag of the country with which they are at war, and when Kamehameha listened carefully and understood the true significance of the flag, he told the American not to think him a fool for he has many flags of different European nations in his stores and so, if the English one is no good, he can raise a different one. After this incident he at once expressed a desire to have his own flag which the English designed for him.

The exact time when this first Hawaiian flag appeared is not known, but another Russian, Captain Kotzebue, sailing in the Russian corvette *Rurik,* found the flag flying over Honolulu when he was there in 1816.

Because there was no written Hawaiian language at this time there has come down no contemporary, native document bearing on the subject. Hawaiian was not reduced to a written language until after the arrival of missionaries in 1820.

So far as is known, the first Hawaiian description of the flag appeared in the government newspaper, *The Polynesian,* in 1845, when it had eight stripes. Some years later the Hawaiian newspaper *Kuokoa,* on January 1, 1862, carried a story on the history of the flag and a picture of it in color. This story, which it appears was not questioned at the time, although there were many persons living in the islands who must have known the facts, is of sufficient interest to reproduce here the pertinent part:

> The Hawaiian flag was designed for King Kamehameha I, in the year 1816. As the King desired to send a vessel to China, to sell a cargo of sandal wood, he, in company of John Young, Isaac Davis, and Captain Alexander Adams, made this flag for the ship, which was a war vessel called the *Forester,* carrying 16 guns, and was owned by King Kamehameha I.
>
> The Flag having been made, the vessel sailed for Macao, China, where the flag was not credited nor recognized as a government flag . . .

Captain Adams, who commanded the *Forester,* did indeed have trouble obtaining recognition of the flag at Macao as the port officials at first refused to permit him to dock, but the payment of exorbitant harbor dues overcame his difficulty. Captain Adams, who was an advisor to King Kamehameha, is believed to have played the dominant role in designing this first flag.

Some students of the subject, however, credit Captain George C. Beckley, another British subject who had sometime earlier sold his vessel to King Kamehameha and had remained in the islands as a friend and advisor of the King, with having been most important in determining the flag's design. Some accounts say that this first flag after long use was given to Captain Beckley and remained in his family, used as a child's dress for many years, but eventually was worn out and discarded.

This flag is reputed to have had the British Union Jack in the upper left hand field with right alternating red, white, and blue stripes from the top to the bottom. But it is not known whether the union of the flag contained the Cross of St. Patrick which was added to the British Union Jack after 1801, and which was not in the "jack" when Captain Vancouver gave Kamehameha his first flag. There is also some controversy whether the stripes numbered seven, eight, or nine.

The colors of the stripes may have been a concession to the three colors of the United States flag, and their pattern resembled that of the stripes in the American flag. The number of stripes, later standardized at eight after 1843, if indeed they had ever been different from that in number, represented the eight principal islands in the Hawaiian group—Oahu (location of the capital city of Honolulu), Maui, Kauai, Hawaii, Molokai, Lanai, Niihau, and Kahoolawe. Of these islands today, the first six are highly developed and choice vacation land;

Niihau is privately owned. Kahoolawe is uninhabited.

United States influence in Hawaiian affairs increased steadily after 1820. On March 31 of that year the first group of Protestant New England missionaries arrived in the islands. In the next thirty-five years, fourteen other missionary groups arrived.

Within about ten years after the flag was first introduced, it became known in the United States. In 1826 the *Waverly* and two other ships flying the Hawaiian flag came into the California ports and thus opened up a new channel of trade.

In 1842, during the reign of King Kamehameha III, the British consul at Honolulu started a violent dispute by claiming valuable land in the city. When the King resisted his claims he sent for help, claiming a dangerous state of affairs existed in the islands. Answering the consul's plea, Lord George Paulet arrived in a British frigate, the *Carysfort*. He intended to seize the islands. Paulet's naval guns and his threats forced the King provisionally to cede his kingdom to Lord Paulet for Great Britain. On February 25, 1843, the Hawaiian flag came down. Lord Paulet apparently had all the Hawaiian flags assembled and destroyed them. No flag of that period survives.

Responding to the King's appeal for help in this situation, Commodore Lawrence Kearny brought the United States frigate *Constellation* into Honolulu harbor. He ordered a Hawaiian flag to be made and hoisted it to his frigate's masthead. William Paty who was present on this occasion wrote in his journal on July 7, 1843, "Today the young Chiefs visited the *Constellation* and on leaving the ship we had the pleasure of seeing the Old *Sandwich Island Flag* flying once more. A flag made on purpose for this occasion was hoisted at the frigate's 'fore' and saluted in good style."

A few days after this event British naval forces arrived at Honolulu under the command of Admiral Richard Thomas, commander of the British navy in the Pacific. Although the British Union Jack still flew on land at the Hawaiian capital, the British protested to the King that he must not allow himself to be saluted under any flag (referring apparently to the flag hoisted on the *Constellation*) other than the British.

But then in a grand and impressive ceremony on July 31, 1843, on the plain east of Honolulu, Admiral Thomas read a proclamation which undid Lord Paulet's action in February by stating that Her Majesty's Government desired King Kamehameha to be treated as an independent sovereign, and he restored to him his kingdom and the independence of the Hawaiians. Thomas lowered the Union Jack and raised the old Hawaiian flag at what is now known as Thomas Square.

It was in this ceremony that in some inadvertent way the flag made for the occasion had the stripes appear in white-red-blue order from the top, instead of red-white-blue, which appears to have been the order in the earlier flags. This mistake was never corrected, and the order and relationship of the stripes in the Hawaiian flag followed that example thereafter.

Dating from the Thomas flag-raising in July 1843, the number of stripes in the flag became standardized at eight. The flag is described in chapter 10 of the 1896 Hawaii statutes as follows:

> The national ensign shall consist of eight horizontal stripes, alternating white, red, blue, etc., beginning at the top, having a jack cantoned in the dexter chief angle next to the point of suspension. The jack shall consist of a blue field charged with a compound saltire of alternate tinctures white and red, the white having precedence; a narrow edge of white borders each red side of the saltire. A red cross bordered with white is charged over all. The jack is half the hoist and 7/16 the fly in length. The arms of the red cross shall be equal in width to one of the horizontal stripes; the white border shall be one third the width of the red cross.

A color plate published at the time gave the proportions of the arms of the compound saltire as equal in width to the red cross, and the colors white and red and the border being in proportion of 3,2, and 1, respectively. This compound saltire includes the Crosses of St. Patrick, St. Andrew, and St. George. This Hawaiian union, in contrast to the British practice with the "union jack" may not be used alone as the Hawaiian flag nor as a "jack" in the bows of vessels.

There were abortive efforts by the French to seize the Hawaiian Islands in 1849 and 1851. In the latter year the Hawaiian king had a secret proclamation prepared which called for placing the islands under the protection of the United States. When the French learned of this they retracted, but during all these threats the Hawaiian flag had continued to fly over the capitol.

In 1854 negotiations were proceeding for United States annexation of the islands but the death of the King ended this.

By 1887 United States influence in the islands was reflected in the exclusive right to enter Pearl Harbor and maintain there a coaling and naval station. American planter and commercial interests had increased in Hawaii with the passing of years, until by 1890 they were a powerful factor in the islands' economy and politics. Divergent local interests and politics brought on a crisis in the kingdom in 1893.

In that year a revolution, instigated and manipulated largely by American interests in the islands with the help of the United States Minister John L. Stevens, overthrew the government of Queen Liliuokalani. United States marines landed. Amid threats of violence and bloodshed, the Queen was deposed on January 17, 1893, and she relinquished her rule to a provisional government.

The Provisional Government requested United States Minister Stevens to declare the islands a United States protectorate. He did so on February 1, 1893, and on that date raised for the first time the United States flag over the Hawaiian Islands. The revolutionary Provisional Government and Minister Stevens opened negotiations with the United States for the annexation of the islands.

President Harrison signed the treaty to accomplish this, but before the Senate acted President Grover Cleveland took office and withdrew the treaty document.

Queen Liliuokalani's protest against the use of United States troops in overthrowing her government caused President Cleveland to order an investigation of the whole affair. Upon its completion, he ordered the kingdom restored to the Queen. Thus, after a lapse of two months, the American flag was lowered and the Hawaiian flag raised once again on April 1 to fly over the islands.

With this turn of events, the revolutionists took things into their own hands. They refused to obey President Cleveland's edict and, led by Sanford B. Dole, forced the Queen to abdicate. On July 4, 1894, they formed the Republic of Hawaii with Dole as president. The new republic retained the old Hawaiian flag as its banner. In the next year there was an unsuccessful insurrection in the islands against the government. In succeeding months several foreign governments and the United States recognized the Republic of Hawaii.

The movement for annexation to the United States had not died, and finally on July 7, 1898, Congress passed a joint resolution authorizing annexation. On August 12, the islands were transferred to the jurisdiction of the United States. The Hawaiian flag flew over the republic for the last time on that day. Thereafter the flag, unchanged, became the territorial flag. It was not until April 30, 1900, however, that Congress passed the organic act establishing the territory of Hawaii, providing for its government as a full-fledged United States territory, and granting citizenship to its people.

When Hawaii became the fiftieth State on August 21, 1959, the old Hawaii territorial flag became the State flag, being recognized as such by Article XIII, Section 3, of the State constitution. As the State flag it flies over public buildings of Hawaii.

Surely this flag has a history that is one of the longest and most colorful relating to any of the flags still surviving and associated with the United States of America.

CHAPTER 19 ★

The Confederate Flags

THE NATIONAL FLAGS OF THE CONFEDERATE STATES of America are included for discussion and illustration in this book because they symbolize the South's united effort to achieve separate national independence in the Civil War. Although unsuccessful, that great movement was nonetheless heroic, and under the Confederate flags thousands of brave Americans fought and died.

On March 4, 1861, in Montgomery, Alabama, a new flag appeared over the State Capitol, meeting place of the Provisional Confederate Congress (Pl. XXIV-57). As bands played and cannon boomed in salute, the Stars and Bars of the Confederate States of America told the world of Southern determination to break the bonds of union with the North.

This first Confederate National Flag, one of dozens of designs considered by a "Committee on a Proper Flag for the Confederate States of America," retained the red, white, and blue of the Flag of the United States. It displayed a red stripe at top and bottom, with a white stripe between them. The union in the upper left corner was blue, with a circle of seven white stars representing the States then comprising the infant Confederacy. More stars could be added as other Southern States followed their sisters out of the Union. This flag was never formally adopted by the Congress, but it was accepted as the official standard of the Confederacy.

In this first stirring season of secession the Stars and Bars appeared throughout the Confederacy, from Virginia to Texas. But while Southerners cheered their new flag, the march of events brought ever closer the time when they would have to shed their blood to defend it. In Virginia, on a hot July day in 1861, the untrained armies of

North and South clashed on the rolling hills above a little stream called Bull Run, less than thirty miles from Washington. Fighting was confused as green troops blundered together in the swirl of battle. At a distance the Confederacy's Stars and Bars could not be distinguished from the flags of the Union forces, and errors of identification compounded the confusion of the war's first great battle. Fortune favored the Confederates, and near the end of that long bloody day the defeated army in blue streamed back toward the national capital of the Union.

Even as they basked in the glow of this first victory, Confederate commanders were aware of the need for a new banner to carry in battle: one which could not be mistaken for that of the enemy. General Joseph E. Johnston, commanding the main Confederate force in Virginia, called on his army for suitable designs. One among several proposals forwarded by General P. G. T. Beauregard was selected, and in a short time a new Battle Flag floated over gray ranks in every theater of war (Pl. XXIV-58). Sometimes known as the "Southern Cross," it is today the most familiar of the Confederacy's standards, although it supplanted the Southern national emblem only on the battlefield.

The Battle Flag was square, in specified sizes for infantry, artillery, and cavalry. It consisted of a red field, emblazoned with a blue St. Andrew's cross having thirteen white stars representing the States the Confederacy claimed as her own. The cross and the red field were bordered in white. Some regiments modified the size and shape of the flag or carried their own distinctive standards, but throughout the war the "Southern Cross" was the most common battle flag carried by the men in gray.

While the Battle Flag followed the Southern armies in the field, the Stars and Bars remained the Confederate National Flag until 1863. There had been agitation in many quarters for a new emblem—one which bore no similarity to the Stars and Stripes of the Union. On May 1, 1863, the Confederate Congress adopted a new design consisting of a white field with the Battle Flag displayed in the upper left corner (Pl. XXIV-59). This standard, too, had its faults, for when furled or draped it resembled a flag of truce or surrender. Still, no changes were made for almost two years until, in the Confederacy's waning days, President Jefferson Davis, on March 4, 1865, approved an act revising the 1863 design.

This last banner of the Confederacy (Pl. XXIV-60) was similar to the one adopted on May 1, 1863, the only major change being the addition of a red bar extended the width of the white field at the end opposite the union. By the time of its adoption the fortunes of the South were ebbing swiftly; Appomattox was only a few weeks away.

Although the political unity they symbolized had but a short and embattled existence, the flags of the Confederacy are proud relics of a cause for which thousands of valiant men fought and died. The national heritage is brighter for the tattered banners which, even in defeat, speak eloquently to the present of American courage and devotion in the past.

Plate XXIII

54

Lone Star Flag of Texas, adopted January 25, 1839, as the official flag of the Republic of Texas. When Texas became the 28th State in the United States on December 29, 1845, this flag continued in use as the State banner.

55

California Bear Flag. This flag is said to be an exact replica of the original raised at Sonoma on June 14, 1846, which was burned in the great San Francisco fire of April, 1906, when the collections of the Society of California Pioneers were destroyed. This replica was made to fly in the June, 1896, semi-centennial celebration of the Bear Flag revolt at Sonoma. It measures 36½ by 58 inches overall. *Photograph Courtesy Sonoma Mission State Historical Monument, California*

56

The Hawaii State Flag of today is identical with the Territorial Flag and the flag of the Republic of Hawaii. It is also identical with the earlier flag of the Hawaiian Kingdom with one exception. In 1843, because of an inadvertent mistake, a white stripe replaced a red one at the top beginning the series, thus reversing the original position of the red and white stripes. The Hawaiian flag was designed apparently in the period 1812-1814 by a British subject working with advisors of King Kamehameha I. The British Union Jack occupies the field in the upper left corner. The eight white, red, and blue stripes represent the eight principal Hawaiian Islands. Their colors apparently were selected because of United States influence. *Photograph Courtesy Hawaii Visitors Bureau*

54

55

56

57
Confederate National Flag (1st), raised on March 4, 1861, over the State Capitol at Montgomery, Alabama, meeting place of the Provisional Confederate Congress. The seven stars in the union at the upper left corner represented the States then in the Confederacy.

58
Confederate Battle Flag, 1861. In the first battle of Bull Run (Manassas), July 21, 1861, the Confederate National Flag at a distance could not be distinguished from the northern flag. This led to a demand for a battle flag that could not be mistaken. General Beauregard submitted the winning design. The 13 stars represented the States claimed by the Confederacy. This flag was sometimes called "The Southern Cross."

59
Confederate National Flag (2nd), adopted May 1, 1863. This flag replaced the first Confederate National Flag because of criticism that the latter resembled the United States Stars and Stripes in some respects. The new Confederate Flag had the disadvantage that it could be mistaken for a flag of truce or surrender.

60
Confederate National Flag (3rd), adopted March 4, 1865.

Part IV

FURTHER INFORMATION ABOUT THE FLAG

★

Alphabetical List of States and Dates of Their Ratification of the Constitution or Admission into the Union

THE THIRTEEN ORIGINAL STATES CREATED THE UNION and became part of it when the Declaration of Independence was signed on July 4, 1776. In the table below, therefore, they are indicated by an asterisk, and the date following the name of each such State is that on which it ratified the Constitution. In every other case, the date given is that of admission to the Union.

Alabama, Dec. 14, 1819
Alaska, Jan. 3, 1959
Arizona, Feb. 14, 1912
Arkansas, June 15, 1836
California, Sept. 9, 1850
Colorado, Aug. 1, 1876
* Connecticut, Jan. 9, 1788
* Delaware, Dec. 7, 1787
Florida, March 3, 1845
* Georgia, Jan. 2, 1788
Hawaii, Aug. 21, 1959
Idaho, July 3, 1890
Illinois, Dec. 3, 1818
Indiana, Dec. 11, 1816
Iowa, Dec. 28, 1846
Kansas, Jan. 29, 1861
Kentucky, June 1, 1792
Louisiana, April 30, 1812
Maine, March 15, 1820
* Maryland, April 28, 1788
* Massachusetts, Feb. 6, 1788
Michigan, Jan. 26, 1837
Minnesota, May 11, 1858
Mississippi, Dec. 10, 1817
Missouri, Aug. 10, 1821
Montana, Nov. 8, 1889
Nebraska, March 1, 1867
Nevada, Oct. 31, 1864
* New Hampshire, June 21, 1788
* New Jersey, Dec. 18, 1787
New Mexico, Jan. 6, 1912
* New York, July 26, 1788
* North Carolina, Nov. 21, 1789
North Dakota, Nov. 2, 1889
Ohio, March 1, 1803
Oklahoma, Nov. 16, 1907
Oregon, Feb. 14, 1859
* Pennsylvania, Dec. 12, 1787
* Rhode Island, May 29, 1790
* South Carolina, May 23, 1788
South Dakota, Nov. 2, 1889
Tennessee, June 1, 1796
Texas, Dec. 29, 1845
Utah, Jan. 4, 1896
Vermont, March 4, 1791
* Virginia, June 25, 1788
Washington, Nov. 11, 1889
West Virginia, June 20, 1863
Wisconsin, May 29, 1848
Wyoming, July 10, 1890

Chronological Table of States and Data on Authorized Flags of the United States*

Order of Ratification or Admission	State	Date Ratified or Admitted	Flag Design	Dates in Use	No. of Stars	No. of Stripes
1	Delaware	Dec. 7, 1787				
2	Pennsylvania	Dec. 12, 1787				
3	New Jersey	Dec. 18, 1787				
4	Georgia	Jan. 2, 1788				
5	Connecticut	Jan. 9, 1788				
6	Massachusetts	Feb. 6, 1788				
7	Maryland	April 28, 1788				
8	South Carolina	May 23, 1788	1st	1777-1795	13	13
9	New Hamphsire	June 21, 1788				
10	Virginia	June 25, 1788				
11	New York	July 26, 1788				
12	North Carolina	Nov. 21, 1789				
13	Rhode Island	May 29, 1790				
14	Vermont	March 4, 1791				
15	Kentucky	June 1, 1792				
16	Tennessee	June 1, 1796				
17	Ohio	March 1, 1803				
18	Louisiana	April 30, 1812	2nd	1795-1818	15	15
19	Indiana	Dec. 11, 1816				
20	Mississippi	Dec. 10, 1817	3rd	July 4, 1818	20	13
21	Illinois	Dec. 3, 1818	4th	July 4, 1819	21	13
22	Alabama	Dec. 14, 1819	5th	July 4, 1820	23	13
23	Maine	March 15, 1820				

24	Missouri	Aug. 10, 1821	6th	July 4, 1822	24	13
25	Arkansas	June 15, 1836	7th	July 4, 1836	25	13
26	Michigan	Jan. 26, 1837	8th	July 4, 1837	26	13
27	Florida	March 3, 1845	9th	July 4, 1845	27	13
28	Texas	Dec. 29, 1845	10th	July 4, 1846	28	13
29	Iowa	Dec. 28, 1846	11th	July 4, 1847	29	13
30	Wisconsin	May 29, 1848	12th	July 4, 1848	30	13
31	California	Sept. 9, 1850	13th	July 4, 1851	31	13
32	Minnesota	May 11, 1858	14th	July 4, 1858	32	13
33	Oregon	Feb. 14, 1859	15th	July 4, 1859	33	13
34	Kansas	Jan. 29, 1861	16th	July 4, 1861	34	13
35	West Virginia	June 20, 1863	17th	July 4, 1863	35	13
36	Nevada	Oct. 31, 1864	18th	July 4, 1865	36	13
37	Nebraska	March 1, 1867	19th	July 4, 1867	37	13
38	Colorado	Aug. 1, 1876	20th	July 4, 1877	38	13
39	North Dakota	Nov. 2, 1889				
40	South Dakota	Nov. 2, 1889				
41	Montana	Nov. 8, 1889	21st	July 4, 1890	43	13
42	Washington	Nov. 11, 1889				
43	Idaho	July 3, 1890				
44	Wyoming	July 10, 1890	22nd	July 4, 1891	44	13
45	Utah	Jan. 4, 1896	23rd	July 4, 1896	45	13
46	Oklahoma	Nov. 16, 1907	24th	July 4, 1908	46	13
47	New Mexico	Jan. 6, 1912	25th	July 4, 1912	48	13
48	Arizona	Feb. 14, 1912				
49	Alaska	Jan. 3, 1959	26th	July 4, 1959	49	13
50	Hawaii	Aug. 21, 1959	27th	July 4, 1960	50	13

* This table indicates the numerical order and date on which each State either ratified the Constitution or was admitted to the Union. It also shows which officially authorized Flag of the United States was in use at the time, together with the number of stars and stripes in its design. The first thirteen States listed ratified the Constitution and were the original States.

Pledge of Allegiance to the Flag

I pledge allegiance to the Flag of the United States of America and to the Republic for which it stands, one Nation under God indivisible, with liberty and justice for all.

WHEN GIVING THE PLEDGE, ONE SHOULD STAND erect with the right hand placed over the heart, fingers together and horizontal with the arm. At the conclusion of the pledge, the arm should be lowered to the side. One should face the flag when pledging allegiance to it.

The Pledge of Allegiance to the Flag was first published in the *Youth's Companion* for September 8, 1892, in connection with the National Public Schools Celebration of Columbus Day in October of that year. At the same time it was printed in leaflet form and distributed throughout the country. More than twelve million public school children all over the United States took the pledge during the celebration of 1892. Mr. Francis Bellamy, of Rome, New York, and Mr. James Upham, of Alden, Massachusetts, were both members of the staff of the *Youth's Companion* when it published the pledge. Mr. Bellamy also served as chairman of the executive committee which prepared the program for the celebration and furnished much of the publicity which attended it.

The family and descendants of both Mr. Bellamy and Mr. Upham subsequently claimed that each of them wrote the pledge. In 1939 the United States Flag Association appointed a committee to determine the disputed question of authorship, so that it could be stated in future with historical accuracy. This committee consisted of two historians, Charles C. Tansill and Bernard Mayo, and one political scientist, W. Reed West. They studied the evidence submitted by the two contending families, and on May 18, 1939, decided the evidence indicated that Francis Bellamy was the author. Their finding was accepted by the American Flag Committee.

When first published, the Pledge of Allegiance contained the phrase "my flag." This wording was criticized on the ground that foreign-born children and adults, when giving the pledge, might have in mind swearing allegiance to the flag of their native land. In order to eliminate this possibility, the First National Flag Conference, held in Washington, D.C., on June 14, 1923, recommended and adopted a change in the wording, substituting for "my flag" the phrase "the Flag of the United States."

A further change in the pledge was made by House Joint Resolution 243, approved by President Eisenhower on June 14, 1954 (Pub. Law 396, 83d Cong., 2d Sess.). This amended the language by adding the words "under God," so that it now reads "one Nation under God indivisible, with liberty and justice for all."

The American's Creed

I believe in the United States of America as a Government of the people, by the people, for the people; whose just powers are derived from the consent of the governed; a democracy in a republic, a sovereign Nation of many sovereign States; a perfect union, one and inseparable, established upon those principles of freedom, equality, justice, and humanity for which American patriots sacrificed their lives and fortunes.

I therefore believe it is my duty to my country to love it; to support its constitution; to obey its laws; to respect its flag; and to defend it against all enemies.

THE AMERICAN'S CREED QUOTED ABOVE WAS WRITTEN in 1918 by William Tyler Page, of Friendship Heights, Maryland, in the course of a nation-wide contest on the subject. Henry Sterling Chapin, of New York, had conceived the contest as a means of promoting the writing of a national creed which would be the briefest possible summary of our political faith based on the fundamental ideas and events of American history and tradition. The then Mayor of Baltimore, James H. Preston, offered a reward of $1,000 for the winning statement. He thought it would be appropriate for the birthplace of Francis Scott Key's "The Star-Spangled Banner" to do this.

One Sunday in May, 1917, while the contest was in progress, Mr. Page conceived the general outline for his draft of a creed. He had long been a student of American history, and was thus familiar with the outstanding events, the great documents, and the pronouncements of illustrious Americans in the nation's past. Working on his draft from day to day, he made many changes, until it was finally completed to his satisfaction. In the ultimate wording he used passages and phrases from many of the great documents of American history, including the Declaration of Independence, the Preamble to the Constitution, Lincoln's Gettysburg Address, and Webster's Reply to Hayne.

In August, 1917, Mr. Page sent his proposed creed to the committee on manuscripts for the contest. Six months later, in March, 1918, the committee notified him that he was the successful competitor among more than three thousand contestants. On April 3 following, in the House of Representatives Building in Washington, D.C., Mayor Preston presented Mr. Page with the award of $1,000. The Commissioner of Education and the Speaker of the House of Representatives accepted the creed on behalf of the United States. The proceedings of this ceremony are recorded in the *Congressional Record,* No. 102, for April 13, 1918. It is interesting to note that Mr. Page bought Liberty Bonds with the award money three days after receiving it, and then gave these bonds to his church.

The meaning of the creed is perhaps best expressed in its author's own words. Mr. Page said of it:

> The American's Creed is a summing up in one hundred words, of the basic principles of American political faith. It is not an expression of individual opinion upon the obligations and duties of American citizenship or with respect to its rights and privileges. It is a summary of the fundamental principles of American political faith as set forth in its greatest documents, its worthiest traditions, and by its greatest leaders.

William Tyler Page was a descendant of John Page, who came to America in 1650 and settled at Williamsburg, Virginia. He spent practically all his adult life in the service of the United States Government at the Capitol, starting to work there as a page on December 19, 1881, when thirteen years of age. In 1919 he was elected Clerk of the House of Representatives, and held that office until December, 1931. A new post, Emeritus Minority Clerk, was then created for him. He occupied it for the remainder of his life.

For twenty-two consecutive years Mr. Page led the assembled Continental Congresses of the Daughters of the American Revolution in reciting the creed. His last public appearance was on Sunday evening, October 18, 1942, when, as a guest of the Daughters of the American Revolution, he led the recitation of The American's Creed at the fiftieth anniversary celebration of the Pledge of Allegiance to the Flag. Mr. Page died the next day.

Part V

USE AND DISPLAY OF THE STARS AND STRIPES

The Code of Flag Display and Use (Public Law 829)

In everyday life individuals conform more or less closely to a code of conduct which constitutes good manners, without which our relationships with one another would become unbearably crude and confused. So too our conduct toward the flag, symbolizing the nation itself, is governed by a code of rules conveniently termed flag etiquette.

Colonel James Moss, founder and president of the former United States Flag Association, argued that knowledge of proper use and display of the flag was a simple matter. As one would not show disrespect to the portrait of one's mother, he observed, neither would one manifest disrespect toward the national emblem. Unfortunately, however, such a general principle of conduct does not help the average person very much. Although one may not need to be told that the flag must never be mutilated or defaced, many situations are bound to arise where correct procedure can be interpreted in different ways. The purpose of flag etiquette is to resolve such differences with uniformity and good sense.

Apart from the armed services, observance of such etiquette is chiefly voluntary, since the Federal Government has until recently seldom attempted to prescribe conduct toward the Stars and Stripes, and even when so doing has provided no penalties for violations thereof. Yet established convention is frequently more binding upon the individual than laws formally enacted. Some of the rules of good manners are obviously of slight importance in themselves, nor is there universal agreement concerning them. Others may be of trivial significance or have disputed validity. How fully they should be observed each person must determine for himself. All this granted, however, a code of some kind is still needed for guidance.

The code of flag etiquette, as it is known today, is a comparatively recent development, in which such agencies as the United States Flag Foundation, the American Legion, and the Daughters of the American Revolution, among others, have played leading roles. The armed forces of the United States have also had an important part in its growth through the years. On June 14, 1923, representatives of some sixty-eight patriotic and civic organizations convened in Washington, D.C., under the auspices of the National Americanization Commission of the American Legion, to draft a uniform code of flag etiquette. Shortly before this, on February 15 immediately preceding, the War Department issued a circular on the rules of flag usage, and these were adopted almost in their entirety by that conference. Since the group never met again, its code as adopted in 1923 remained the acceptable standard for many years, being subsequently published by the Adjutant General's Office of the War Department, along with certain additional data, as an eight-page pamphlet.

Finally, in 1942, Congress assumed the task of bringing together "existing rules and customs pertaining to the display and use of the flag of the United States of America." The results of its labors were embodied in a joint resolution approved December 22 of that year. This being the most detailed and complete statement on the subject now in existence, it is here printed in full, and also graphically illustrated, as the code by which all Americans should be guided in connection with either official or personal etiquette where the Stars and Stripes is concerned:

[PUBLIC LAW 829—77TH CONGRESS]
[CHAPTER 806—2D SESSION]
[H. J. Res. 359]
JOINT RESOLUTION

To amend Public Law Numbered 623, approved June 22, 1942, entitled "Joint resolution to codify and emphasize existing rules and customs pertaining to the display and use of the flag of the United States of America".

Resolved by the Senate and House of Representatives of the United States of America in Congress Assembled, That Public Law Number 623, approved June 22, 1942, entitled "Joint resolution to codify and emphasize existing rules and customs pertaining to the display and use of the flag of the United States of America", be, and the same is hereby amended to read as follows:

That the following codification of existing rules and customs pertaining to the display and use of the flag of the United States of America be, and it is hereby, established for the use of such civilians or civilian groups or organizations as may not be required to conform with regulations promulgated by one or more executive departments of the Government of the United States.

SEC. 2. (a) It is the universal custom to display the flag only from sunrise to sunset on buildings and on stationary flagstaffs in the open. However, the flag may be displayed at night upon special occasions when it is desired to produce a patriotic effect.

(b) The flag should be hoisted briskly and lowered ceremoniously.

(c) The flag should not be displayed on days when the weather is inclement.

(d) The flag should be displayed on all days when the weather permits, especially on New Year's Day, January 1; Inauguration Day, January 20; Lincoln's Birthday, February 12; Washington's Birthday, February 22; Army Day, April 6; Easter Sunday (variable); Mother's Day, second Sunday in May; Memorial Day (half staff until noon), May 30; Flag Day, June 14; Independence Day, July 4; Labor Day, first Monday in September; Constitution Day, September 17; Columbus Day, October 12; Navy Day, October 27; Armistice Day, November 11; Thanksgiving Day, fourth Thursday in November; Christmas Day, December 25; such other days as may be proclaimed by the President of the United States; the birthdays of States (dates of admission); and on State holidays.

(e) The flag should be displayed daily, weather permitting, on or near the main administration building of every public institution.

(f) The flag should be displayed in or near every polling place on election days.

(g) The flag should be displayed during school days in or near every schoolhouse.

SEC. 3. That the flag, when carried in a procession with another flag or flags, should be either on the marching right; that is, the flag's own right, or, if there is a line of other flags, in front of the center of that line.

(a) The flag should not be displayed on a float in a parade except from a staff, or as provided in subsection (i).

(b) The flag should not be draped over the hood, top, sides, or back of a vehicle or of a railroad train or a boat. When the flag is displayed on a motorcar, the staff shall be fixed firmly to the chassis or clamped to the radiator cap.

(c) No other flag or pennant should be placed above or, if on the same level, to the right of the flag of the United States of America, except during church services conducted by naval chaplains at sea, when the church pennant may be flown above the flag during church services for the personnel of the Navy.

How to Display

Sec. 2 (d) On Memorial Day

Sec. 3 (d) With Another Flag on Crossed Staffs

Sec. 3 (f) On Same Halyard with Flags of Cities and Organizations

Sec. 3 (g) With Flags of Two or More Nations

Sec. 3 In Procession

Sec. 3 (e) Grouped with Flags of Other Nations and States

Sec. 3 (h) On Staff at Angle from Building

Sec. 4 (d) Display of Bunting

Sec. 3 (h) Suspended over Sidewalk

Sec. 3 (j) Over Middle of Street

Sec. 3 (k) In Church

Sec. 5 Salute to the Flag

Sec. 3 (i) On Wall

Sec. 3 (k) On Speaker's Platform

Sec. 3 (l) When Unveiling a Statue

Sec. 3 (n) Draped over Casket

(d) The flag of the United States of America, when it is displayed with another flag against a wall from crossed staffs, should be on the right, the flag's own right, and its staff should be in front of the staff of the other flag.

(e) The flag of the United States of America should be at the center and at the highest point of the group when a number of flags of States or localities or pennants of societies are grouped and displayed from staffs.

(f) When flags of States, cities, or localities, or pennants of societies are flown on the same halyard with the flag of the United States, the latter should always be at the peak. When the flags are flown from adjacent staffs, the flag of the United States should be hoisted first and lowered last. No such flag or pennant may be placed above the flag of the United States or to the right of the flag of the United States.

(g) When flags of two or more nations are displayed, they are to be flown from separate staffs of the same height. The flags should be of approximately equal size. International usage forbids the display of the flag of one nation above that of another nation in time of peace.

(h) When the flag of the United States is displayed from a staff projecting horizontally or at an angle from the window sill, balcony, or front of a building, the union of the flag should be placed at the peak of the staff unless the flag is at half staff. When the flag is suspended over a sidewalk from a rope extending from a house to a pole at the edge of the sidewalk, the flag should be hoisted out, union first, from the building.

(i) When the flag is displayed otherwise than by being flown from a staff, it should be displayed flat, whether indoors or out, or so suspended that its folds fall as free as though the flag were staffed.

(j) When the flag is displayed over the middle of the street, it should be suspended vertically with the union to the north in an east and west street or to the east in a north and south street.

(k) When used on a speaker's platform, the flag, if displayed flat, should be displayed above and behind the speaker. When displayed from a staff in a church or public auditorium, if it is displayed in the chancel of a church, or on the speaker's platform in a public auditorium, the flag should occupy the position of honor and be placed at the clergyman's or speaker's right as he faces the congregation or audience. Any other flag so displayed in the chancel or on the platform should be placed at the clergyman's or speaker's left as he faces the congregation or audience. But when the flag is displayed from a staff in a church or public auditorium elsewhere than in the chancel or on the platform it shall be placed in the position of honor at the right of the congregation or audience as they face the chancel or platform. Any other flag so displayed should be placed on the left of the congregation or audience as they face the chancel or platform.

(l) The flag should form a distinctive feature of the ceremony of unas the covering

be first hoisted to the
alf-staff position. The flag
is lowered for the day. By
ne-half the distance between the
mers may be affixed to spear heads
a parad of the President of the United States.

(n) When the flag is cover a casket, it should be so placed that the union is at the head and over the left shoulder. The flag should not be lowered into the grave or allowed to touch the ground.

SEC. 4. That no disrespect should be shown to the flag of the United States of America; the flag should not be dipped to any person or thing. Regimental colors, State flags, and organization or institutional flags are to be dipped as a mark of honor.

(a) The flag should never be displayed with the union down save as a signal of dire distress.

(b) The flag should never touch anything beneath it, such as the ground, the floor, water, or merchandise.

(c) The flag should never be carried flat or horizontally, but always aloft and free.

(d) The flag should never be used as drapery of any sort whatsoever, never festooned, drawn back, nor up, in folds, but always allowed to fall free. Bunting of blue, white, and red, always arranged with the blue above, the white in the middle, and the red below, should be used for covering a speaker's desk, draping the front of a platform, and for decoration in general.

(e) The flag should never be fastened, displayed, used, or stored in such a manner as will permit it to be easily torn, soiled, or damaged in any way.

(f) The flag should never be used as a covering for a ceiling.

(g) The flag should never have placed upon it, nor on any part of it, nor attached to it any mark, insignia, letter, word, figure, design, picture, or drawing of any nature.

(h) The flag should never be used as a receptacle for receiving, holding, carrying, or delivering anything.

(i) The flag should never be used for advertising purposes in any man-
er whatsoever. It should not be embroidered on such articles as cushions
handkerchiefs and the like, printed or otherwise impressed on paper
ins or boxes or anything that is designed for temporary use and dis-
or used as any portion of a costume or athletic uniform. Advertising
ould not be fastened to a staff or halyard from which the flag is

THE
such
destr
ony
de

(j) The flag, when it is in [illegible] emblem for display, should be [illegible] burning.

SEC. 5. That during the ceren[illegible] when the flag is passing in a para[illegible] should face the flag, stand at attent[illegible] form should render the military salut[illegible] [illegible]m, remove the headdress with the right ha[illegible] at the le[illegible], the hand being over the heart. Men withou[illegible] should salute in the same manner. Aliens should stand at attention. Women should salute by placing the right hand over the heart. The salute to the flag in the moving column should be rendered at the moment the flag passes.

SEC. 6. That when the national anthem is played and the flag is not displayed, all present should stand and face toward the music. Those in uniform should salute at the first note of the anthem, retaining this position until the last note. All others should stand at attention, men removing the headdress. When the flag is displayed, all present should face the flag and salute.

SEC. 7. That the pledge of allegiance to the flag, "I pledge allegiance to the flag of the United States of America and to the Republic for which it stands, one Nation (under God) indivisible, with liberty and justice for all", be rendered by standing with the right hand over the heart. However, civilians will always show full respect to the flag when the pledge is given by merely standing at attention, men removing the headdress. Persons in uniform shall render the military salute.

SEC. 8. Any rule or custom pertaining to the display of the flag of the United States of America, set forth herein, may be altered, modified, or repealed, or additional rules with respect thereto may be prescribed, by the Commander in Chief of the Army and Navy of the United States, whenever he deems it to be appropriate or desirable; and any such alteration or additional rule shall be set forth in a proclamation.

Approved, December 22, 1942.

(j) The flag, when it is in such condition that it is no longer a fitting emblem for display, should be destroyed in a dignified way, preferably by burning.

Sec. 5. That during the ceremony of hoisting or lowering the flag or when the flag is passing in a parade or in a review, all persons present should face the flag, stand at attention, and salute. Those present in uniform should render the military salute. When not in uniform, men should remove the headdress with the right hand holding it at the left shoulder, the hand being over the heart. Men without hats should salute in the same manner. Aliens should stand at attention. Women should salute by placing the right hand over the heart. The salute to the flag in the moving column should be rendered at the moment the flag passes.

Sec. 6. That when the national anthem is played and the flag is not displayed, all present should stand and face toward the music. Those in uniform should salute at the first note of the anthem, retaining this position until the last note. All others should stand at attention, men removing the headdress. When the flag is displayed, all present should face the flag and salute.

Sec. 7. That the pledge of allegiance to the flag, "I pledge allegiance to the flag of the United States of America and to the Republic for which it stands, one Nation (under God) indivisible, with liberty and justice for all", be rendered by standing with the right hand over the heart. However, civilians will always show full respect to the flag when the pledge is given by merely standing at attention, men removing the headdress. Persons in uniform shall render the military salute.

Sec. 8. Any rule or custom pertaining to the display of the flag of the United States of America, set forth herein, may be altered, modified, or repealed, or additional rules with respect thereto may be prescribed, by the Commander in Chief of the Army and Navy of the United States, whenever he deems it to be appropriate or desirable; and any such alteration or additional rule shall be set forth in a proclamation.

Approved, December 22, 1942.

veiling a statue or monument, but it should never be used as the covering for the statue or monument.

(m) The flag, when flown at half staff, should be first hoisted to the peak for an instant and then lowered to the half-staff position. The flag should be again raised to the peak before it is lowered for the day. By "half staff" is meant lowering the flag to one-half the distance between the top and bottom of the staff. Crepe streamers may be affixed to spear heads or flagstaffs in a parade only by order of the President of the United States.

(n) When the flag is used to cover a casket, it should be so placed that the union is at the head and over the left shoulder. The flag should not be lowered into the grave or allowed to touch the ground.

SEC. 4. That no disrespect should be shown to the flag of the United States of America; the flag should not be dipped to any person or thing. Regimental colors, State flags, and organization or institutional flags are to be dipped as a mark of honor.

(a) The flag should never be displayed with the union down save as a signal of dire distress.

(b) The flag should never touch anything beneath it, such as the ground, the floor, water, or merchandise.

(c) The flag should never be carried flat or horizontally, but always aloft and free.

(d) The flag should never be used as drapery of any sort whatsoever, never festooned, drawn back, nor up, in folds, but always allowed to fall free. Bunting of blue, white, and red, always arranged with the blue above, the white in the middle, and the red below, should be used for covering a speaker's desk, draping the front of a platform, and for decoration in general.

(e) The flag should never be fastened, displayed, used, or stored in such a manner as will permit it to be easily torn, soiled, or damaged in any way.

(f) The flag should never be used as a covering for a ceiling.

(g) The flag should never have placed upon it, nor on any part of it, nor attached to it any mark, insignia, letter, word, figure, design, picture, or drawing of any nature.

(h) The flag should never be used as a receptacle for receiving, holding, carrying, or delivering anything.

(i) The flag should never be used for advertising purposes in any manner whatsoever. It should not be embroidered on such articles as cushions or handkerchiefs and the like, printed or otherwise impressed on paper napkins or boxes or anything that is designed for temporary use and discard; or used as any portion of a costume or athletic uniform. Advertising signs should not be fastened to a staff or halyard from which the flag is flown.

of a long-established local custom or under the authority of the language of the Joint Resolution of December 22, 1942, which states that "the flag may be displayed at night upon special occasions when it is desired to produce a patriotic effect." This language has not been the subject of strict interpretation or regulation. The "special occasion" has by practice in some places become "day and night." Among the places known to fly the flag at night in addition to the two in Baltimore already mentioned are the following:

East and West Fronts of the Central Section of Capitol Building, Washington, D.C. (beginning in 1918)
Birthplace of Francis Scott Key, Keysville, Maryland
Grave of Francis Scott Key, Mount Olivet Cemetery, Frederick, Maryland
Municipal War Memorial, Worcester, Massachusetts
Marine Monument, Quantico, Virginia
Little Bighorn Battlefield, Montana
The Plaza, Taos, New Mexico
Mount Stover, Colton, California
Pike's Peak, Colorado
Mount Suribachi, on the island of Iwo Jima, in the Pacific

Of the above places, special comment may be of interest concerning three of them. The Municipal War Memorial Auditorium in Worcester, Massachusetts, constructed in 1933, was designed with the idea of flying the flag there twenty-four hours a day. The flag was raised opposite the auditorium on November 11, 1933, on a ninety-foot flagstaff set in a bronze and granite base, and it has been flying there ever since.

The Stars and Stripes apparently has flown longest, day and night, at Taos, New Mexico. It appears that Kit Carson, in 1861, assisted by Captain Smith H. Simpson of the United States Army, nailed a Union Flag to a pole in the plaza at Taos as a symbol that citizens of New Mexico were loyal to the Union. Vigilance was maintained during the Civil War years to see that the flag flew there day and night. The practice traditionally has been observed ever since.

Atop Mount Suribachi, on the little island of Iwo Jima in the western Pacific, the Stars and Stripes waves day and night to honor the United States Marines who planted it there in World War II.

Display of the Stars and Stripes at Night

THERE ARE TWO PLACES IN THE UNITED STATES where the Stars and Stripes is flown at night by specific legal authority (as of January, 1960). At all other places where it is flown at night authority is derived from interpretation of the Joint Resolution of Congress described in Public Law 829 (see pp. 160-166), or from previously established custom.

The three instances in which the flag is flown at night by specific authority, two in Baltimore, Maryland, are the following:

1. Under authority granted in the Joint Resolution of December 22, 1942, President Truman, on July 2, 1948, issued a proclamation stating that, "as a perpetual symbol of our patriotism, the flag of the United States shall hereafter be displayed at Fort McHenry National Monument and Historic Shrine at all times during the day and night, except when the weather is inclement."

2. Public Law 319, approved March 26, 1954 (56 Stat. 377; 36 USC 175) permits the flying of the United States Flag twenty-four hours of each day at the Flag House, Flag House Square, East Pratt Street, Baltimore.

3. Under authority granted in the Joint Resolution of December 22, 1942 (56 State. 1074), President Kennedy, on June 12, 1961, issued a proclamation stating that "the flag of the United States of America shall hereafter be displayed at the United States Marine Corps Memorial in Arlington, Virginia, at all times during the day and night, except when the weather is inclement." This Memorial, often popularly known as the Iwo Jima Memorial, portrays members of the United States Marine Corps raising the flag over Mt. Suribachi on Iwo Jima, February 23, 1945.

At other places where the flag is flown at night it is done because

Marking of Aircraft with the United States Flag

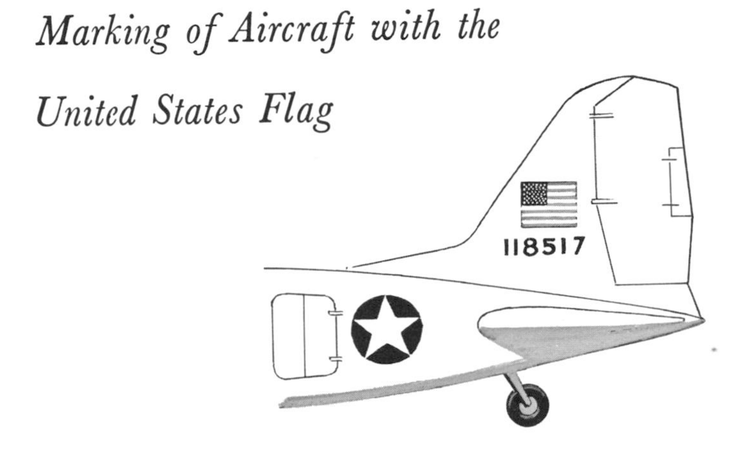

Current air force practice requires identification of aircraft assigned to air attachés to be marked with the United States Flag. The instructions for marking are as follows:

The standard marking will be an American flag painted on both sides of the vertical stabilizer, either above, below or forward of the radio call number. The using organization commander may choose the exact location on the vertical stabilizer for the flag, giving due consideration to eye appeal and balance. The flag will be positioned horizontally and in such manner that the union will be uppermost. The bars of the flag will appear to be trailing at all times. If possible, the flag should be 2 feet high and 3.8 feet long for C-47 and larger aircraft. For smaller aircraft, the size of the flag will be reduced proportionately.

Use of New and Superseded Flags

The white house, on August 21, 1959, issued the following statement governing the use of the new fifty-star flag and of the forty-nine-star and forty-eight-star flags which it supersedes:

By law, the new 50-star flag will become the official flag of the United States on July 4, 1960, the birthday of the Union. Display of the new flag before that time would be improper. However, it would not be improper to display the 48-star flag or the 49-star flag after that date; with limited exceptions agencies of the Federal Government will continue to display the 48-star flag and the 49-star flag so long as they remain in good condition and until existing stocks of unused flags are exhausted. It is appropriate for all citizens to do the same.

Notes to Part I

INTRODUCTION (pp. 19-20)

1. The real Philip Nolan was an American trader and filibusterer from Kentucky, whose career was quite different, and whose name Hale chose almost by accident for that of his hero. For details, see the following: Edward Everett Hale, "The Real Philip Nolan," Mississippi Historical Society *Publications,* Vol. IV (1901), pp. 281-329; "Expeditions of Nolan," in J. T. Adams, ed., *Dictionary of American History,* Vol. IV (New York: 1940), p. 137; and "Philip Nolan (c. 1771-Mar. 21, 1801)," in Dumas Malone, ed., *Dictionary of American Biography,* Vol. XIII (New York: 1934), pp. 543-544.

2. Cf. similar comment in William Elliot Griffis, *The American Flag of Stripes and Stars* (Ithaca, no date), in connection with usage of the flag in Revolutionary War days.

CHAPTER 1 BEFORE THE STARS AND STRIPES (pp. 23-28)

1. For this proclamation, see William G. Perrin, *British Flags, Their Early History and Their Development at Sea, with an Account of the Origin of the Flag as a National Device* (Cambridge: 1922), p. 55.

2. *Ibid.*

3. John H. Fow, in *The True Story of the American Flag* (Philadelphia: 1908), pp. 14-15, observes that such an American flag was never seen or heard of by anyone. Mr. R. C. Ballard Thruston, scholarly author of *The Origin and Evolution of the United States Flag* (Washington: 1926), comments that an artist depends for income on selling his work, and therefore usually makes it salable, even at the expense of historical facts. Trumbull's paintings are no exception to this general rule.

4. Compare Milo M. Quaife, *The Flag of the United States* (New York: 1942). See also Frank Earle Schermerhorn, *American and French Flags of the Revolution, 1775-1783* (Pennsylvania Society of Sons of the Revolution, Philadelphia: 1948); and Gherardi Davis, *Regimental Colors in the War of the Revolution* (New York: 1907), and *Supplement* thereto (New York: 1910). Unfortunately, Schermerhorn's text is uncritical in many respects.

5. Contemporary descriptions of the ceremony are printed in Alfred M. Cutler, *The Continental "Great Union" Flag* (Somerville: 1929), pp. 26-28.

6. Fow, *op. cit.,* p. 26.
7. For further references, see Quaife, *op. cit.,* p. 58.
8. Reproduced in *The National Geographic Magazine,* Vol. XXXII, p. 288.
9. Cutler, *op. cit.,* p. 30.

CHAPTER 2 A NEW CONSTELLATION (pp. 29-35)

1. Compare Thruston, *op. cit.,* for similar comment.

2. Peleg D. Harrison, *The Stars and Stripes and Other American Flags, . . .* (5th edit., Boston: 1914), p. 64.

3. Italics supplied by the present authors. For the correspondence, see Gherardi Davis, *The Colors of the United States Army, 1789-1912* (New York: 1912), pp. 3-7; also printed in an article by Alexander J. Wall in New-York Historical Society *Quarterly Journal,* Vol. XVII, pp. 51-67.

CHAPTER 3 THE FATHER OF THE STARS AND STRIPES (pp. 36-40)

1. Col. James A. Moss, *The Flag of the United States* (Washington, D.C.: 1941), p. 40.

2. For the story of Hopkinson's career, see George E. Hastings, *The Life of Francis Hopkinson* (Chicago: 1926).

CHAPTER 4 THE STARS AFLOAT (pp. 41-47)

1. Francis Wharton, ed., *The Revolutionary Diplomatic Correspondence of the United States* (Washington, Government Printing Office: 1947), p. 63.

2. Mrs. Reginald de Koven, *The Life and Letters of John Paul Jones,* Vol. I (New York: 1913), pp. 282-83.

3. See Milo M. Quaife's discussion with Prof. Charles Lewis about Jones's answer to Pearson in the *Mississippi Valley Historical Review,* Vol. XIX, pp. 401-06.

4. Also previously published in *The American Heritage Book of the Revolution* (New York: 1958), p. 289.

5. For a discussion of this and other early printed depictions of the flag, see Lawrence Wroth's *Annual Report* of the John Carter Brown Library, 1950-51, pp. 38-47.

6. On the origin of trade to the Northwest Coast and China see Joseph Schafer, *The Pacific Coast and Alaska,* in *History of North America,* Vol. X (Philadelphia: 1914), Chapter II; also Samuel E. Morison, *The Maritime History of Massachusetts, 1783-1860* (Boston: 1921), Chapters IV-VII.

7. For the original journals of the voyages of the *Columbia,* see Frederic W. Howay, ed., *Voyages of the "Columbia" to the Northwest Coast, 1787-1790 and 1790-1793,* in Massachusetts Historical Society *Collections,* Vol. LXXIX (Boston: 1941).

CHAPTER 5 FIRST HONORS ON LAND (pp. 48-53)

1. John Spargo, *The Stars and Stripes in 1777: An Account of the Birth of the Flag and Its First Baptism of Victorious Fire* (Bennington Battle Monument and Historical Association, Bennington, Vt.: 1928), p. 17.

2. *Ibid.,* pp. 17-18.

3. James Phineas Baxter, ed., *The British Invasion from the North. The Campaigns of Generals Tarleton and Burgoyne from Canada, 1776-1777, with the Journal of Lieut. William Digby, of the 53d, or Shropshire Regiment of Foot* (Albany, N.Y.: 1887), pp. 234-35.

4. Spargo, *op. cit.*, pp. 18-30. The quotation is from pp. 29-30.

5. *Ibid.*, pp. 37-48.

6. *Ibid.*, pp. 46-47.

7. *Ibid.*, p. 49.

8. See full-color illustration in *The American Heritage Book of the Revolution,* p. 255.

9. Spargo, *op. cit.*, pp. 49-54.

10. Quaife, *op. cit.*, p. 76. A color photograph of this flag also appears in Lonnelle Aikman, "New Stars for Old Glory," *The National Geographic Magazine,* Vol. CXVI, p. 94.

11. Quaife, *op. cit.*, p. 76-77.

12. *Ibid.*, p. 77, note 3.

13. The quotation is from a letter dated May 14, 1958, addressed to Melvin J. Weig by Charles E. Hatch, Jr., Chief, Research and Interpretation Division, Colonial National Historical Park, Yorktown, Va., following his examination of the original watercolor at Williamsburg.

14. Hugh F. Rankin, "The Genesis of the American Flag, Its Growth, Design, and Triumph at Yorktown, 1776-1781," a research report prepared in typewritten form for the National Park Service, U.S. Department of the Interior, April 4, 1952, has a well-documented section on the case for the Stars and Stripes at Yorktown, pp. 59-65. The evidence supporting the text statement above is Edward M. Riley, ed., "St. George Tucker's Journal of the Siege of Yorktown, 1781," *William and Mary Quarterly,* 3rd ser., Vol. V (July, 1948), p. 385.

15. Rankin, *op. cit.*, p. 62, citing the diaries and journals of Capt. Joseph McClellan, Lt. William Feltman, and Lt. William McDowell, all of the Pennsylvania Line, in *Pennsylvania Archives,* 2nd ser., Vol. XI, p. 698, and Vol. XV, p. 303.

16. Rankin, *op. cit.*, p. 63, citing *The Journal of a Bayreuth Soldier, Johann Conrad Doehla, during the North American War for Independence, 1777-1785* (Bayreuth: 1913), p. 159-60. Rankin says this incident was also reported by another German mercenary in Joseph Rosengarten, ed., *Popp's Journal, 1777-1783* (Philadelphia: reprinted from the *Pennsylvania Magazine of History and Biography,* 1902), p. 24.

17. Bauman's plan of Yorktown is also reproduced in full color in *The American Heritage Book of the Revolution,* p. 370.

18. Information received from Mr. Richard Koke, Curator of The New-York Historical Society, New York City, which has a considerable collection of Bauman manuscripts.

19. Reproduced in color in *The American Heritage Book of the Revolution,* p. 371.

20. See *The National Geographic Magazine,* Vol. CXVI, p. 100; and *The American Heritage Book of the Revolution,* p. 344.

CHAPTER 6 THE SECOND STARS AND STRIPES (pp. 54-62)

1. Massachusetts, Connecticut, New York, Virginia, North Carolina, South Carolina, and Georgia.

2. Since the Iroquois tribes resided chiefly in New York, and sovereignty over them had been asserted earlier by England, that State laid claim to all the region, extending westward to the Mississippi, which the Iroquois had overrun, chiefly in the seventeenth century.

3. The future States of Ohio, Indiana, Illinois, Michigan, and Wisconsin.

4. For the above summary of legislative debates and actions, see *Annals of the Congress of the United States* (Washington: 1834-56), Vol. IV, pp. 19 and following.

CHAPTER 7 THE STAR-SPANGLED BANNER (pp. 63-69)

1. Oscar G. T. Sonneck, *Report on the "Star-Spangled Banner"* . . . (Washington: 1909). Strangely enough, Sonneck took no note of the narrative of John S. Skinner, Key's companion when the song was written, as first published in the Baltimore *Patriot,* May 23, 1849, and subsequently in the *National Intelligencer,* June 4, 1849, and in the *Maryland Historical Magazine* for December, 1937 (Vol. XXXVII, pp. 340-47). The text account above is based mainly upon Sonneck's Report and Skinner's old-age recital.

2. Nicholson was a brother-in-law of Mrs. Key. See the account in Harold I. Lessem and George C. Mackenzie, *Fort McHenry National Monument and Historic Shrine, Maryland,* National Park Service Historical Handbook Series, No. 5 (Washington, D.C.: 1950), p. 21. This study is excellent for some additional details and illustrations pertinent to the entire subject under discussion.

3. *Maryland Historical Magazine,* Vol. XXXVII, p. 349.

4. Lessem and Mackenzie, *op. cit.* p. 23.

5. Quaife, *op. cit.,* pp. 112-13. See also Lessem and Mackenzie, *op. cit.,* p. 23.

6. These verses are printed in Sonneck, *op. cit.,* p. 39.

7. Printed in his *The Flag of the United States* (Chicago: 1931), Vol. II, p. iv.

CHAPTER 8 THE THIRD STARS AND STRIPES (pp. 70-79)

1. George H. Preble, *Origin and History of the American Flag* . . ., new edition in two volumes, Vol. I (Philadelphia: 1917), p. 343.

2. *Ibid.,* Vol. I, p. 345.

3. 35th Congress, 2nd Session, House Document 160, February 5, 1859.

4. Preble, *op. cit.,* Vol. I, pp. 342-45.

5. Captain Reid had also submitted a design for a "national standard," which he proposed to be flown over the halls of Congress, navy yards and arsenals, and at other public places visited by the President of the United States, during his presence. This was not adopted. Preble says it was "composed of the emblematic representations of our escutcheon quartered upon it: viz., the stars, white on a blue field on the upper left-hand quarter; the Goddess of Liberty on a white field under the stars; the eagle in the upper right-hand

quarter or fly of the standard on a white field; and the thirteen alternate stripes of red and white under the eagle." See Preble, *op. cit.*, Vol. I, p. 343, where there is also an illustration of such a standard with the stars arranged in four parallel, horizontal rows of five each.

6. *Ibid.*, Vol. I, p. 349.

7. *Ibid.*, Vol. I, p. 347.

CHAPTER 9 EARLY UNITED STATES ARMY FLAGS (pp. 80-86)

1. William A. Ganoe, *The History of the United States Army* (New York and London: 1924), pp. 90-95.

2. Thruston, *op. cit.*, pp. 12-15.

3. Wayne Papers, printed in Sons of the American Revolution, *National Year Book* for 1916, pp. 219-20.

4. Preble, *op. cit.*, Vol. II, pp. 491-93.

5. Quaife, *op. cit.*, pp. 134-35.

6. Quaife, *op. cit.*, pp. 137-38 and note 9.

7. On all these and related flags of the early American military establishment, perhaps the most helpful reference work is Davis, *Colors of the United States Army*. See especially, in addition to the text, his black-and-white Plate I facing p. 3, color Plate II facing p. 11, and color Plate III facing p. 12, for examples of the regimental colors described above. Quaife, *op. cit.*, has a somewhat less detailed color reproduction of the 4th Infantry regimental color, Plate VII, Fig. 37, facing p. 98.

8. Thruston, *op. cit.*, pp. 15-16 and Fig. 17.

CHAPTER 10 THE STARS JOIN THE ARMY (pp. 87-93)

1. For detailed discussion and illustration of these and other flags described in this chapter, see Davis, *op. cit.;* also Quaife, *op. cit.*, particularly Plate VII, facing p. 98. In the latter, Figs. 38 and 40 are erroneously transposed.

2. Davis, *op. cit.*, p. 42.

3. Quaife, *op. cit.*, pp. 144-45, stated that this flag was preserved and has a color illustration of it (Plate VII, Fig. 38, facing p. 98). Davis, *op. cit.*, color Plate VII, facing p. 27, also pictures the banner. However, Mr. Roy E. Appleman recently engaged in extensive correspondence in a concerted effort to find the original of the flag, extending all the way to Alaska and many Army depots and installations throughout the United States, all to no avail.

4. See illustrations in Davis, *op. cit.*, black-and-white Plate X, top, facing p. 42 (reversed photograph); and Quaife, *op. cit.*, Plate VII, Fig. 41, facing p. 98. Quaife's is a color reproduction. Davis (p. 43) comments that this flag was typical of all artillery colors used from 1834 until the new regulations were issued.

5. On the complicated subject of the 1862 introduction, to both the artillery and the cavalry, of guidons made like the national flag, with stars and stripes, see Col. W. A. Graham, "The Colors of the Seventh at the Battle of the Little Big Horn," published in the 1950 Los Angeles Westerners' *Brand Book*, and reissued by the author as a pamphlet in 1952.

6. General Order No. 93, November 26, 1866, cited in Davis, *op. cit.*, p. 51.

7. Color illustrations are in *ibid.,* Plate XIII, facing p. 52; and Quaife, *op. cit.,* Plate VII, Fig. 42, facing p. 98.

8. General Order No. 34, May 29, 1886, cited in Davis, *op. cit.,* p. 55.

9. General Order No. 31, April 13, 1887, cited in *ibid.,* p. 56

10. Statement of R. C. Ballard Thruston to Milo M. Quaife, made in letter of January 15, 1941, based upon an examination of the correspondence between Gherardi Davis and the War Department, and upon inspection of the original orders issued in 1895. Thruston concluded: "I think the orders, mentioned by Gherardi Davis, were issued in 1887, were not carried into effect, and new orders were issued in 1895. But I have never been able to get any admission of the correctness of that supposition from the War Department."

11. Davis, *op. cit.,* pp. 63-67.

12. Bernard J. Tremain, ms. history of the United States Flag in the library of the Filson Club, Louisville, Ky., p. 213.

13. *Ibid.* Thruston, *op. cit.,* p. 19, and Fig. 20.

CHAPTER 11 SOME STORIES AND LEGENDS (pp. 94-102)

1. Canby's paper was never published, and the manuscript is not known to be in existence, according to a letter of May 4, 1942, addressed to Milo M. Quaife by B. J. Johnstone on behalf of the society. The Ross story has been told so many times, and by so many different family spokesmen, that numerous variations and embellishments of detail have entered into the various relations of it. For what may perhaps be regarded as its final presentation, by an intelligent representative of the family, see Lloyd Balderston, *The Evolution of the American Flag* (Philadelphia: 1909).

2. Since Washington lived in Virginia and Mrs. Ross in Philadelphia, one cannot help wondering when, and under what circumstances, this prior relationship was established.

3. This is also mentioned by Joseph Jackson in his *Encyclopedia of Philadelphia* (Harrisburg: 1931-33), Vol. 4, p. 1055.

4. Augustus C. Buell, *Paul Jones, Founder of the American Navy,* 2 vols. (New York: 1900). The author's perversions begin with the very title of his book, for Jones was in no sense the founder of our Navy, even though he became one of its most brilliant ornaments. For authoritative exposures of Buell's biography, see address of Prof. A. B. Hart, published in *American Historical Review,* Vol. XV, pp. 231-32; and Mrs. Reginald De Koven, *A Fictitious Paul Jones Masquerading as the Real* (pamphlet, no imprint and no date, but consisting in part of a reprint copyrighted by the *New York Times* in 1904).

5. Buell, *op. cit.,* Vol. I, p. 80.

6. For the story of the Portsmouth maidens, see *ibid.,* Vol. I, pp. 244-45; and Vol. II, p. 78.

7. Willis F. Johnson, *The National Flag* (Boston and New York: 1930), p. 63.

8. The whole fabulous tale is exposed in De Koven, *op. cit.,* pp. 26-27.

9. His report, made to Benjamin Franklin a few days after the battle, along with other contemporary and later accounts, is printed in John H. Sherburne,

Life and Character of the Cavalier John Paul Jones . . . (Washington, D.C.: 1825).

10. For the Stafford family history and claims see New Jersey Historical Society *Proceedings,* Vol. IX, pp. 86-90; and the same, 2nd Series, Vol. II, pp. 191-95; also Preble, *op. cit.,* Vol. I, pp. 281-83.

11. Report made to Milo M. Quaife by Margaret B. Klapthor, then Acting Head Curator of the Department of History, Smithsonian Institution, on June 18, 1956.

12. Line illustration in Preble, *op. cit.,* Vol. I, p. 282. The Stafford banner is also pictured in Harlan H. Horner, *The American Flag* (New York Department of Education, Albany: 1910), p. 53.

13. The printed facsimile appears in Preble, *op. cit.,* Vol. I, p. 281. The Pennsylvania Historical Society's transcript was attested by William S. Stryker, former Adjutant General of New Jersey, on May 9, 1876.

14. See also correspondence of the Curator of History at the Smithsonian with Cyrus T. Brady, printed in the latter's *Commodore Paul Jones* (New York: 1928), pp. 467-69.

15. Preble, *op. cit.,* Vol. I, pp. 267-69.

CHAPTER 12 MORE FICTIONS AND MYTHS (pp. 103-108)

1. Telfair M. Menton, "The Origin of the American Flag," *Journal* of the Society for Army Historical Research, Vol. 8 (January, 1929), pp. 114-20. An ancient Scottish legend relates that King Malcolm I, on the eve of the battle of Brunanbaugh in 937, saw the cross of St. Andrew in the clear blue sky and adopted it as the national emblem.

2. Col. James A. Moss, *The American Flag: Its Glory and Its Grandeur* (United States Flag Association, 1st edit.: 1929), pp. 22-25.

3. For this and other interpretations of the significance of colors in the flag, see Robert Phillips, *The American Flag: Its Uses and Abuses* (Boston: 1930), pp. 54-55.

4. 5th edit., 5th printing: 1952.

5. Letter from Miss Heilman, Chief Bibliographer, to Milo M. Quaife.

6. Benson J. Lossing, *Mount Vernon and Its Associations, Historical, Biographical, and Pictorial* (A. S. Hale & Co., Hartford, Conn.: 1870), pp. 27-28.

7. His most successful work, *Proverbial Philosophy,* was first published in 1838 and by 1881 had sold over 1,000,000 copies in the United States—an astonishing achievement, considering the country's wealth and population at that time.

8. Aldrich's address was reported in the New York *Herald-Tribune* (Paris edition), September 29, 1955; and also in the New York *World,* September 28, 1955.

9. Executive Order No. 10834, signed by President Eisenhower, August 21, 1959. See reference in *Federal Register,* Vol. 24, No. 166.

10. For example, see Col. W. H. Waldron, *Flags of America* (Huntington, W. Va.: 1935), p. 24, where a diagram of the stars in the flag is accompanied by a key, headed "Know the Star that Represents Your State on the Flag." The idea that the original thirteen States entered the Union in the order of their

ratification of the Constitution is set forth in Myrtle Garrison, *Stars and Stripes* (Caldwell, Idaho: 1941), Chap. VIII. See also Moss, *op. cit.*, p. 23, where the diagram is headed "Pick out the Star of your State," and where the thirteen "cantons" into which the book is divided are dedicated, successively, to the thirteen original States in the order of their "admission" to the Union.

11. See *Annals of Congress,* 15 Cong., 1 sess., House of Representatives, p. 517, as cited in United States Army Regulations, No. 840-10, October 28, 1952.

CHAPTER 13 THE FLAG TODAY (pp. 109-112)

1. President Taft's original order of June 24, 1912, was modified in part by a second executive order (No. 1637) issued October 29, 1912; and again by a third executive order (No. 2390) issued by President Wilson on May 29, 1916.

2. At the direction of President Eisenhower, the flag was raised by Secretary of the Interior Fred A. Seaton. See *First Official Raising of the 49-Star Flag of the United States at Fort McHenry National Monument and Historic Shrine* (National Park Service, U.S. Department of the Interior, program folder, printed courtesy of the Evelyn Hill Corporation).

3. This order was published in full in the *Federal Register,* Vol. 24, No. 166 (issued August 25, 1959), pp. 6865 and 6867.

4. Thus minor variations would be permissible for national colors carried by the armed forces. Commercial dealers in Stars and Stripes flags for general civilian use may still ignore the executive order in details and length of the fly. Dimensions commonly used by such flag manufacturers in former years have been three by five feet, four by six feet, and eight by twelve feet.

Index